Chicken Soup for the Recovering Soul

Daily Inspirations

Jack Canfield, Mark Victor Hansen,
Peter Vegso, Gary Seidler, Tian Dayton,
Rokelle Lerner, Robert J. Ackerman, Ph.D.
and Theresa Peluso

Health Communications, Inc.
Deerfield Beach, Florida

www.hcibooks.com
www.chickensoup.com

We have excerpted passages from the following books:

366 Encouragements for Prosperity ©1992 Yvonne Kaye, Ph.D. Call (215) 393-5464. Visit *www.yvonnekaye.com*.

Chicken Soup for the Nurse's Soul. ©2001 Jack Canfield and Mark Victor Hansen. To order: *www.hci-online.com*.

Chicken Soup for the Recovering Soul ©2004 Jack Canfield and Mark Victor Hansen. To order: *www.hci-online.com*.

Daily Affirmations for Adult Children of Alcoholics ©1985 Rokelle Lerner. To order: *www.hci-online.com*.

(continued on page 372)

Library of Congress Cataloging-in-Publication Data

Chicken soup for the recovering soul : daily inspirations / Jack
    Canfield . . . [et al.].
        p. cm.
    ISBN 0-7573-0318-8
    1. Recovering addicts—Anecdotes.   I. Canfield, Jack, 1944–

HV4998.C45 2005
204'.42—dc22

                                                                    2005056398

©2005 Jack Canfield, Mark Victor Hansen
ISBN 0-7573-0318-8

Publisher: Health Communications, Inc.
3201 S.W. 15th Street
Deerfield Beach, FL 33442–8190

R-01-06

Cover and inside design by Larissa Hise Henoch
Inside formatting by Dawn Von Strolley Grove

When you come to the edge of all the light you have and must take a step into the darkness of the unknown, believe that one of two things will happen to you: Either there will be something solid for you to stand on, or, you will be taught how to fly.

Patrick Overton

Today I have a fresh start. I choose to begin letting go of unhealthy thoughts, feelings and attitudes that have stifled my growth. Today I choose to think new thoughts, to look at new values and to find new ways of expressing my God-given gifts. I now choose to deepen my understanding of others and myself. I will look at my relationships with family and my friends in a new light. I choose to have vital, healthy interactions with others. I truly welcome this new day, this new year and this new me. I welcome the wonderful possibilities open to me.

Rokelle Lerner

Be like a sponge when it comes to each new experience. If you want to be able to express it well, you must first be able to absorb it well.

Jim Rohn

Footnotes for Life

_____

_____

_____

_____

_____

_____

_____

_____

JANUARY 2

When I grew up, I learned not to rock the boat; asserting my own opinions and desires could get me in trouble. Sometimes I carry this over in my parenting; I don't take a stand or set limits. When my children push or threaten to get angry, the fear I felt as a child comes up and my reaction is to placate them and keep the peace. This is not healthy. I need to feel those fears I felt as a child along with the sense of helplessness that overwhelmed me. I need to separate myself as a child from myself as an adult. I also need to separate my inner child from the child I am raising.

Tian Dayton

Loving a child doesn't mean giving in to all his whims; to love him is to bring out the best in him, to teach him to love what is difficult.

Nadia Boulanger

Footnotes for Life

_____

_____

_____

_____

_____

_____

_____

When I was a teen, my grandmother taught me how to cross-stitch. I was apprehensive at first, sure that my disability would interfere. It always did. My grandmother reassured me that I could do simple patterns at my own pace.

There were curses; there were smiles. There were times I quit and times I began again. But when I completed my first pattern I realized the mistakes and curses were twined with perfect stitches and smiles to create something brand new. Just like life.

It's a lesson I re-learn every time I thread a needle.

Christyna Hunter

Great is the art of beginning, but greater is the art of ending.

Henry Wadsworth Longfellow

Footnotes for Life

_____

_____

_____

_____

_____

_____

_____

_____

JANUARY 4

Spend a few minutes, a few hours, or an entire day unconcerned about what others will think, or what's in it for you, or whether something offends you or not.

Feel the freedom, delight in the ability to accomplish, and explore possibilities that you may never before have even known about.

Once you decide to let go of your ego, it's a very simple thing to do. And it will truly change your world for the better.

Brahma Kumaris
World Spiritual University

Detachment is being close to what you most want to be free from and using it to make you grow.

Brahma Kumaris

Footnotes for Life

_____

_____

_____

_____

_____

_____

Just for today, I will not hate.

Just for today, I will forgive the one who hurt me. I will remember that I am a child of God, and I will take the child out to play.

Just for today I will ask God to forgive me, and just for today, I will let Him.

Jaye Lewis

*Forgiveness is a gift
you give yourself.*

Suzanne Somers

Footnotes for Life

_____

_____

_____

_____

_____

_____

_____

_____

Within every human being there is an inherent sense of dignity and self-respect. Circumstances in life might cause it to be buried under layers of grime but sooner or later, this sense of dignity pushes its way up for recognition and one day breaks through the surface. That's the day a person becomes aware that "I am too good for this." At that moment, the miracle of recovery can begin.

Abraham J. Twerski

The best solution for little problems is to help people with big problems.

Rabbi Kalman Packouz

Footnotes for Life

_____

_____

_____

_____

_____

_____

_____

Embrace life and all it has to offer, then you can live with an appreciation for all it's worth. When you embrace life there is a sense of satisfaction and contentment that comes over you, helping you to live each moment with acceptance and gratitude. Not always longing to be someplace else or wishing for something different. Instead you are taking what comes your way and turning it into the best it can be. You can live with a purpose, enjoying every moment, and with a thankfulness that stirs in you a deeper commitment to embrace life even more.

Peggy Reeves

There's only us, there's only this, forget regret, or life is yours to miss. No other road, no other way, no day but today.

Jonathan Larson

Footnotes for Life

_____

_____

_____

_____

_____

_____

_____

_____

When I was alone and hope seemed so far away, I met a soul who changed my life–myself. I began to learn, to love, to be responsible for my future and to accept that the past cannot be changed.

Rather than walk without direction, lost inside my tormented mind, I learn and accept that if I feel pain, I can feel joy as well. I can enjoy the present and cherish a sunset, a lake, a tear, a smile, a friend.

Isa Traverso-Burger

I can't change the direction of the wind, but I can adjust my sails to always reach my destination.

Unknown

Footnotes for Life

_____

_____

_____

_____

_____

_____

_____

_____

The more I recognize abundance as being meant for me, the more it will be true. An unconscious attitude of limitation and scarcity will find its way into my life if I allow it to. When I can see the prosperity in this world as a boundless supply, one in which I partake along with others, I open the channels for it to enter into my life. I will think positively about other people's prosperity, knowing that what I believe to be true for someone else, I also believe to be true for me. I accept the abundance in my life.

Tian Dayton

The moon belongs to everyone; the best things in life are free.

B.G. DeSylva

Footnotes for Life

_____

_____

_____

_____

_____

_____

_____

_____

Dreams are surprisingly durable. Though forgotten, they will lie like dry seeds buried in desert sands, waiting. A dream may appear fragile and lifeless, but inside the parched husk waits lush creative potential. We sometimes forget these old dreams of ours, but they do not forget us. Spring rains arrive at last, following the hard years of drought, and our "dead" dreams sprout most unexpectedly. We are filled with delight to see their long-forgotten shape, to breathe their fragrance again, and we wonder at our carelessness in forgetting. Today, I will visit my garden of forgotten dreams . . . and bring a watering can.

All our dreams can come true . . . if we have the courage to pursue them.

Walt Disney

Rhonda Brunea

Footnotes for Life

The harsh winter winds call attention to themselves, and I am mindful of all the unpleasant aspects of the unfriendliest of seasons. Some memories of my unhappy childhood still linger within me, blowing icy blasts through my soul. I am aware of these, just as I am aware of the chill in the world around me. There is no need to struggle against these elements. I am as unique and important to life's scheme as each snowflake. I have a new and abiding warmth in my soul as I patiently await the coming of spring with its warmth, sunshine and fresh breezes to rejuvenate me.

Rokelle Lerner

What life means to us is determined not so much by what happens to us as by our reaction to what happens.

Lewis L. Dunnington

Footnotes for Life

_____

_____

_____

_____

_____

_____

_____

_____

JANUARY 12

Some think he's a little strange. A week before my son was born; I rested against his fence and admired his flowers. He was quiet for a while and said, "I used to watch those through my window when I was in prison." I protectively placed my hand over my unborn child. "I was a prisoner of war," he continued. "Just a kid really. Both my parents and my sister were murdered and I didn't want to live. Then, I saw those cosmos through my cell window and I made up my mind that if I was ever free, I'd go and touch them and keep some of the seeds." Things are not always what they seem.

Mary Lee Moynan

Infinite riches are all around you if you will open your mental eyes and behold the treasure house of infinity within you.

Joseph Murphy

Footnotes for Life

_____

_____

_____

_____

_____

_____

_____

We make extensive lists. We make lists of all that is broken about ourselves; we also have long lists of what we should be doing, and aren't doing yet; we have lists of regrets, lists of complaints, and lists of "it will never happen." But today, let us start a new list entitled *All That Is Possible with Me*. It starts like this: I can hold someone's hand; I can feed the ducks; I can read a book; I can write a book; I can become president; I can feel the cold and the warm; I can color any page blue if I want; I can breathe; I can smile.

Barbara A. Croce

I know of no better life purpose than to perish in attempting the great and the impossible.

Friedrich Nietzsche

Footnotes for Life

_____

_____

_____

_____

_____

_____

_____

JANUARY 14

We are survivors. We are resilient. Within us is great strength, an ability to overcome and to endure. From pain we never deserved, we build walls to hold in our secrets. Secrets that seem too difficult to face head-on. Secrets we fear, if shared, will only bring more pain. You have a choice and you have a voice. Keep your secret locked up within your walls forever, or use your strength and courage to break the silence and allow the truth to set you free.

Nicole Braddock

Truth is the secret of eloquence and of virtue, the basis of moral authority; it is the highest summit of art and of life.

Henri Frederic Amiel

Footnotes for Life

_____

_____

_____

_____

_____

_____

_____

_____

The day after my daughter confessed to me that my husband of ten years was molesting her, I found myself without a home, no job and with three frightened, displaced children in a women's shelter. I had spent ten years dodging shouts and blows, trying to make a nice life out of what had become a nightmare. I had obviously failed. I was as low and lost as I'd ever been. When the counselor asked what choices I had made in my life that had brought me to this moment, it was a turning point. Everything from that day forward would be the result of that long, hard look at myself. It was the first small step for me.

In the depth of winter I finally learned there was, in me, invincible summer.

Albert Camus

Jaye Lewis

Footnotes for Life

_____

_____

_____

_____

_____

_____

_____

JANUARY 16

My recovery lifts my spirit and gives my life a deeper purpose. Even my compulsive behavior was an attempt to grow, to find inner peace, however misguided. But today I recognize that the peace I sought can only truly be found by uniting my will with God's. When I willfully try to push my life in place, I am limited in my vision. Today I invite spirit to involve itself intimately in all the petty arrangements of my life. Nothing is too small for spirit to be a part of. I am one with spirit; separateness is but an illusion, for the very second I invite spirit to be with me, it is there.

Love is faith, and one faith leads to another.

Henri-Frédéric Amie

Tian Dayton

Footnotes for Life

_____

_____

_____

_____

_____

_____

_____

We as a group are privy to knowledge that is rapidly coming to the rest of the world. There is a Spiritual solution to every single problem, question and situation in our lives, because that is what we indeed are, creatures of a Spiritual nature, a Spiritual origin. This is the most important thing that we have learned as a result of working the Twelve Steps.

Jeffrey R. Anderson

Resolve to perform what you ought; perform without fail what you resolve.

Stonewall Jackson

Footnotes for Life

_____

_____

_____

_____

_____

_____

_____

Sobriety is not attained just by putting the cork in the bottle. It is suggested that our emotional growth stopped the day we started drinking and as we acquire more and more sobriety we "catch up." I know that I am addicted to alcohol and am just one drink away from a drunk. For me, staying sober is paramount in my life. Without my sobriety and spirituality I am nothing.

Rev. Bob Lew

Love truth, but pardon error.

Voltaire

Footnotes for Life

_____

_____

_____

_____

_____

_____

_____

Will you please accept the help we're offering? This was the question asked by each of Ruth's family members assembled for the intervention. Ruth's family not only loved her, they revered her. She had a great capacity to give and a way of making people forget their troubles. She was everyone's ray of sunshine. She drank infrequently, but after her husband's heart attack, the binges became more frequent and more dangerous. Ruth looked around the room at her family and through tears, with a small smile the seventy-three-year-old grandmother said, "Yes, I'll accept your help today."

Debra Jay

In spite of warnings, nothing much happens until the status quo becomes more painful than change.

Laurence J. Peter

Footnotes for Life

_____

_____

_____

_____

_____

_____

_____

_____

The problem with using a crutch—alcohol, drugs, food, gambling—to numb our emotional pain is that in the end we come to rely on it instead of on our own inner strength. We learn to lie quite persuasively: "I don't need to drink. I just like the taste." "These pills have caffeine in them. It's like drinking coffee"; "I work hard for my money. I deserve to gamble if it relaxes me."

This above all: to thine own self be true.

William Shakespeare

It becomes easier and easier to convince ourselves that our problems are under control. Eventually, when there are serious consequences and the crutch is no longer available, the only way to regain our health and to remain well is to acknowledge the truth.

Kay Conner Pliszka

Footnotes for Life

_____

_____

_____

_____

_____

_____

_____

Sometimes I find myself living life like a prison sentence—just doing time, trying to stay out of trouble, filling my days with activities and thoughts just for something to do. On those days I have forgotten how it feels to wonder about life; to wonder why we are here, to wonder where we might be going, to wonder how I might contribute. Today I will be curious. I will carry questions in my pockets: What matters most? What can I do to express my gratitude? What can I do for someone I love—or maybe a complete stranger? I want more than a good day in prison. I want a wonder-full life.

Thom Rutledge

Who we are, the kind of people we will be, individually and collectively, is ultimately determined by one thing: how we relate to fear.

Thom Rutledge

Footnotes for Life

_____

_____

_____

_____

_____

_____

_____

_____

JANUARY 22

Worry is rehearsing calamity, meditating on the worst thing that can happen. Worry is a joy stealer and a time robber. Worry sets a tone of unrest to those around you, causing misery to everyone. What is the antidote to worry? Count your blessings. Live one day at a time. Break the habit of negative self-talk.

Take the energy you use in worrying and replace it with overwhelming positive thoughts. See yourself worry free with God's help and then be successful, prosperous and victorious.

Joan Clayton

Being happy today takes care of tomorrow.

Joan Clayton

Footnotes for Life

_____

_____

_____

_____

_____

_____

_____

Change is generally regarded as positive, but it can be destructive as well. When running toward change, ask yourself, "From what am I running?" Are you leaving behind a family, a job, a reputation or troubles that are overwhelming? Change may bring relief and a fresh start but finding happiness and success right where you are may be more challenging and enduring.

Elaine Young McGuire

Change is an easy panacea. It takes character to stay in one place and be happy there.

Elizabeth Clarke Dunn

Footnotes for Life

_____

_____

_____

_____

_____

_____

_____

_____

At times in the past, my love had been hidden, blocked off by impenetrable clouds. No light or love came through. These clouds prevented me from seeing the love within me and the love within someone else. In my family the love we felt for each other often got cloudy with broken promises, fear, anger and confusion. But today, the confusion, anger and fear are gone. I no longer dwell on past broken promises, instead I let my love shine forth and share my gifts with others.

Rokelle Lerner

Take the power to love what you want in life and love it honestly.

Susan Polis Schutz

Footnotes for Life

_____

_____

_____

_____

_____

_____

_____

Alicia was referred to me hoping I might solve the mystery. She was writing poetry with hints of suicide and showing signs of extreme anxiety. Her parents insisted nothing was wrong and refused professional counseling for her. Fortunately, the door to my high school student assistance office was always open. After many weeks Alicia slowly began confiding a lifetime of sexual abuse—from her grandfather and father. Those revelations began a difficult process for Alicia but with her secrets and pain no longer hidden, she faced the truth. It is never too late to begin healing and as Alicia discovered, help can be just down the hall.

> *Not everything that is faced can be changed, but nothing can be changed until it is faced.*
>
> James Baldwin

Kay Conner Pliszka

Footnotes for Life

_____

_____

_____

_____

_____

_____

_____

_____

Regardless of the things that I thought I had gotten away with, I have learned that there are no free rides. Being responsible for my recovery also means being responsible for my actions, as well as the effects that my actions may have on others.

When I made my direct amends to my children, they immediately forgave me—no questions asked. I was grateful for their unconditional forgiveness and in accepting it, know that I must unconditionally forgive those in my life who had wronged me in the past.

Sala Dayo

> *I have not failed. I have merely found 10,000 ways that won't work.*
>
> Thomas Edison

Footnotes for Life

_____

_____

_____

_____

_____

_____

_____

When confronted with impossible and confusing situations, remember three profound thoughts given in four words at many railroad crossings: Stop, Look and Listen.

If we really consider each of those words when dealing with difficulty, even when we're not necessarily negotiating an automobile across a set of railroad tracks, we'd be well on the path of resolution.

Stop and take a deep breath. Look and concentrate on the situation. Listen within yourself or turn to others for guidance.

Bruce Squiers

Everyone should carefully observe which way his heart draws him, and then choose that way with all his strength.

Hasidic Saying

Footnotes for Life

_____

_____

_____

_____

_____

_____

_____

_____

My name is Debbie and I am an alcoholic. I had reached out to A.A. and wanted to make an honest effort to work the Steps but I was a confirmed atheist. One day my sponsor asked me to list all of the characteristics I wanted my Higher Power to have. For several days I considered my list and settled on supportive, caring, forgiving, understanding, patient and non-controlling. One evening as I was driving to a meeting, mentally reviewing my list, I suddenly heard a voice say, "You already have me with you." I immediately felt as though a heavy weight had been lifted off my shoulders. I could stand straight and hold my head up proudly. My name is Debbie and I am in recovery.

I am not a phoenix yet, but here among the ashes, it may be that the pain is chiefly that of new wings trying to push through.

May Sarton

Debbie Heaton

Footnotes for Life

After work I often found myself at the drive-thru window, ordering lots of food and consuming it in my car before going home. When I complained about the grips of my addictive behavior to a wise friend she simply said, "Do something different and you'll get different results." That night I told myself that I wanted to cook a healthy meal. I stopped at the grocery store, got the ingredients and did just that. Occasionally, I still find myself at the drive-thru but I don't beat myself up. I acknowledge how poorly I feel after bingeing and contrast that with the calm I feel after I cook for myself. The pattern is broken.

Lisa Jo Barr

Why not go out on a limb? That's where the fruit is.

Will Rogers

Footnotes for Life

_____

_____

_____

_____

_____

_____

_____

_____

Powerful emotions stir as I recall the places from which I have come. Worlds of seemingly unrecoverable loss and immense pain until his words brought peace and a hand of beauty, love and grace reached into the vile darkness to rescue me. Tears, no longer of rage and anger, roll down my face in thankfulness for the life I have now found.

Sobriety; a life no longer dominated by drugs, alcohol, rage and pain. Each day brings with it the promise of something better, this can only be so as the words he spoke echo somewhere deeply in my soul.

Godwin H. Barton

We are not human beings having a spiritual experience. We are spiritual beings having a human experience.

Pierre Teilhard de Chardin

Footnotes for Life

_____

_____

_____

_____

_____

_____

_____

_____

When I am in a bad mood and feel like blaming someone else for it, I will try something new—I won't. Blaming doesn't work. It makes the other person defensive and deaf to what I say, and it postpones my seeing and understanding what the feeling beneath the blame is. Today I will recognize that beneath my urge to blame is probably either self-condemnation or a fear of being blamed myself. I will stay with those feelings and see what they are about for me before I act on them by blaming someone else.

I will connect with my Higher Power today and see where the connection leads me.

Tian Dayton

Tian Dayton

Footnotes for Life

_____

_____

_____

_____

_____

_____

_____

_____

Early in my recovery A.A. members told me, "Let us love you 'til you can love yourself." I surrendered. As my sobriety grew, they offered, "Don't get too hungry, angry, lonely, tired." I accepted. When they advised, "It's the first drink that gets you drunk, just stay away from that first drink." I understood. When they suggested, "Don't think about not drinking for the rest of your life, only today." I knew. When someone told me, "Don't quit before the miracle." I believed. And when I heard, "Remember alcohol gave you wings to fly but then it took away the sky," I was free. What wise words!

Dorri Olds

Live not one's life as though one had a thousand years, but live each day as the last.

Marcus Aurelius Antoninus

Footnotes for Life

_____

_____

_____

_____

_____

_____

_____

_____

FEBRUARY 2

I was astounded to find myself powerless over my feelings. When I first got sober and started feeling feelings that had been numbed for years, I thought there must be a way to control these feelings away.

My sponsor explained that, along with being powerless over alcohol, people, places and things, I was powerless over my emotions. My life would be unmanageable if I thought I was in charge. After attempts to stuff my feelings using food or avoid them by shopping, I began to be conscious of my powerlessness. Surrendering to powerlessness became my best choice. This let me feel my feelings, process them and live life more fully.

Life is a great big canvas, and you should throw all the paint on it you can.

Danny Kaye

Pamela Knigh

Footnotes for Life

_____

_____

_____

_____

_____

_____

_____

I walk softly with my spirit today. I am uplifted by the thought that I am not alone, nor ever was. I am waiting in pleasant anticipation for spirit to work its quiet magic in my day. There is nothing that I can think, feel or do, that cannot be made lighter and truer by inviting spirit into it. I rest in the joyous awareness that spirit is with me; has never left me. If I feel an absence of spirit I will remember that it is not spirit that moves away from me, but me that moves away from spirit.

Tian Dayton

If you can't have faith in what is held up to you for faith, you must find things to believe in yourself, for a life without faith in something is too narrow a space to live.

Alec Bourne

Footnotes for Life

_____

_____

_____

_____

_____

_____

_____

_____

FEBRUARY 4

My mom often summarized her philosophy in succinct phrases. One of her favorites was:

The most precious gifts should not be kept or hidden.

They should be given freely with no strings; a smile, a kiss and love.

Amelia Rose Bederka
as told to Steve Bederka-Toth

Go out into the world
today and love the
people you meet. Let
your presence light
new light in the hearts
of people.

Mother Teresa

Footnotes for Life

_____

_____

_____

_____

_____

_____

_____

The road to recovery should be renamed the joy of discovery. Each day I uncover a part of me that was lost and hidden from view. I love the transformation as I look forward to my future and the person that I am becoming.

Let me accept today's challenges with gratitude knowing that I will be given the inner strength needed to go on with my life. Not everyone is so fortunate to be given a second chance to start over. Let me see the opportunity in my hardships rather than despair, as the guiding force for goodness leads me there.

Tell me and I'll forget; show me and I may remember; involve me and I'll understand.

Chinese Proverb

Theresa Meehan

Footnotes for Life

_____

_____

_____

_____

_____

_____

_____

_____

FEBRUARY 6

Recovering from my mother's death wasn't easy for me. Because she was elderly, it was generally accepted that her death should be expected but I still missed her. One day while going through her things I found a small journal; inside she had written, "Such a pretty book for pretty thoughts." Apparently she died shortly after, because the following pages were blank. I began on the next page and wrote my memories of her: funny things she said and did and about the life of love she lived. She continues to live through my words not only for myself but also for those that read about her in years to come.

Carol Van Dyke Brown

> *The written word may be our greatest invention. It allows us to converse with the dead, the absent, and the unborn.*
>
> Abraham Lincoln

Footnotes for Life

_____

_____

_____

_____

_____

_____

_____

_____

I had never felt better in my life when during my annual health check-up my doctor delivered stunning news. I had last stage liver disease. In one brief moment everything had changed. In talking with my wife later, I heard myself saying, "Remember that exercise, the one that asked you to consider what regrets you might have if you had only twenty-four hours to live? Well, I can't think of any. All of the people I love know I love them and I know they love and honor me. There's no unfinished business. I feel grateful." Tears of joy began to run down my cheeks. Who would have thought that my journey in recovery would pay off with such dividends?

> *Don't compromise yourself. You're all you've got.*
>
> Betty Ford

Ted Klontz

Footnotes for Life

_____

_____

_____

_____

_____

_____

_____

_____

FEBRUARY 8

I worked on a horse ranch for Anna and Pete every summer until I left home at eighteen. My memories are full of afternoons flying through tall grass holding onto the reins while Fleet Foot, the horse I cared for, did his job cutting cattle. I never told Anna or Pete about the horrors that were going on in my childhood home, but I shared my deepest secrets with Fleet Foot. Those days at the "Flying W" were few but the work I did there was more than cutting cattle and mending fences; the lasting work was the mending of my spirit and the knowledge that we all deserve to be treated with kindness and compassion.

Jane Middelton-Moz

If one is without kindness, how can one be called a human being?

Sarada Devi

Footnotes for Life

_____

_____

_____

_____

_____

_____

_____

Through self-expression we find insight and we begin to understand. Through community with others we find understanding and we begin to heal.

Through releasing of the past we find courage to face the future and we begin to forgive.

Alexandra P.

> *Courage is the price*
> *that life exacts for*
> *granting peace. The*
> *soul that knows it not,*
> *knows no release from*
> *little things.*
>
> Amelia Earhart Putnam

Footnotes for Life

_____

_____

_____

_____

_____

_____

_____

_____

When we were using, we had no problem manipulating our schedules to fit in quality time for our addictions.

Filling the bottomless pit of them constituted a full-time job.

Our new way of life can be free of insanity and frenzy; we can be content to slow down and just be.

Candy Killion

It is time to make the time.

Henry Dumas

Footnotes for Life

_____

_____

_____

_____

_____

_____

_____

_____

Pat had a rough start in the program, relapsing often until he finally "figured it out," as he says. He was a "wrecker" when he drank. He'd tear things apart, knock down walls, leave a mess everywhere he went. Most of his sober time was spent paying for all the damage he caused while on his drinking sprees.

One night during a blacked-out relapse, a tornado came through a town where he was holed up. Cars were turned over, roofs torn off houses, trees uprooted. In the morning when he staggered to the door of the motel and saw the damage, he looked up to the heavens and wailed, "Holy God! How am I going to pay for all this?"

> *Made direct amends to such people wherever possible, except when to do so would injure them or others.*
>
> Step 9, The Twelve Steps of A.A.

As told to Earnie Larsen

Footnotes for Life

_____

_____

_____

_____

_____

_____

_____

_____

FEBRUARY 12

It's amazing we ever get so lost and even more amazing we come back from the realms of addictions, but we do. It is no wonder that, with the insanity of this world, we trust so little and fear so much. That's who I was, one who really trusted very little and feared most of all. During my time in treatment I realized that maybe I wasn't what I did. That who I had been wasn't who I had to be. I could choose again. My program teaches me that knowing what I am doing is nowhere nearly as important as just showing up and letting life show me.

Lee R. McCormick

Answer that you are here—that life exists and identity. That the powerful play goes on, and you may contribute a verse.

Walt Whitman

Footnotes for Life

_____

_____

_____

_____

_____

_____

_____

_____

So often I have wanted to run away but an invisible hand held me in place. I remained, worked through the issue I wanted to escape and I overcame. In the midst of the struggle, I discovered a wonderful truth: I can't lose if I don't give up. Failure is not an option if I don't quit. I intend to win in life. I have made it this far, and I am going to make it all the way. I believe in me.

Barbara A. Croce

That which we persist in doing becomes easier—not that the nature of the task has changed, but our ability to do has increased.

Ralph Waldo Emerson

Footnotes for Life

_____

_____

_____

_____

_____

_____

_____

_____

FEBRUARY 14

Whel it is hard to breathe, slow down. Think of one breath at a time. Relax and drift inward. Focus on happier times with people you love.

Think of how important your life is to others.

Think of your dreams.

Think of tomorrow, next week, next year.

Inhale slowly. Exhale slowly.

Taste the air as it miraculously fills you.

One breath at a time.

Felice Prager

Imagine that you are a Masterpiece unfolding, every second of every day, a work of art taking form with every breath.

Thomas Crum

Footnotes for Life

_____

_____

_____

_____

_____

_____

_____

_____

Talking is a powerful way to share experiences, to create intimacy and build a connection between people. Many of us find it difficult to talk about our feelings, often because we feel so much shame about what we've been through. We are afraid to tell other people what we feel, or what we struggle with. We expect to be rejected or condemned or humiliated.

Share your story with someone today. It takes courage, but we are all human beings who desire acceptance and understanding. All you have to lose is shame and fear.

Lisa Jo Barr

Silent gratitude isn't much use to anyone.

Gladys Berthe Stern

Footnotes for Life

_____

_____

_____

_____

_____

_____

_____

_____

The close of the front door ended the abuse. I watched my husband, once my best friend, and the father of my three children, walk out of our lives. Tears of relief and a trickle of regret emptied down my cheeks. Money was scarce and it was difficult keeping the kids safe and well cared for, but all of those challenges paled in comparison with the peace of mind and the emotional security we felt as soon as the abuse stopped. I drew strength and confidence with each smile on my children's faces and every hug told me any sacrifice was worth giving our family of four another chance.

Cynthia Borris

> *You grow up the day you have your first real laugh—at yourself.*
>
> Ethel Barrymore

Footnotes for Life

_____

_____

_____

_____

_____

_____

_____

When my three-year-old son was diagnosed with autism I made a promise never again to let a day go by that I didn't hug him and tell him I loved him. It no longer mattered if he returned my love or if he continued to push me away. He would never leave this Earth without knowing how much I loved him. I kept my promise and he has done very well. Today he is a very happy, loving little boy and I am a believer in the power of unconditional love.

Linda C. Bird

Being deeply loved by someone gives you strength; loving someone deeply gives you courage.

Lao-tzu

Footnotes for Life

_____

_____

_____

_____

_____

_____

_____

_____

" God, do you know how hard it is for me to love you? Do you know how hurt I am? Do you know that even though I don't understand *why;* why I am an alcoholic—why I had to lose my child. I don't need to know the answers to those questions anymore. In spite of every burden that I carry, either by my own free will or by your command, even though my soul cries for release, even though I will always feel this way—I still love you, God. Though I wanted to blame you and hate you, I love you anyway."

With that prayer, faith, courage, honesty, acceptance and surrender became the foundation of my recovery.

Julie Orlando

> *I want to know God's thoughts. The rest are details.*
>
> Albert Einstein

Footnotes for Life

Believe in your body, it will lead you toward recovery. Your legs will carry you to the meetings when you don't want to go. Your hands will write in the journal every day even if you think you don't have anything to say. Your heart will beat stronger than it ever has because now it beats in a drug-free body. Your soul is your strength to continue to guide you through one day at a time. Your mind will remind you of your past so you don't repeat it. Your eyes will see the future of living a drug-free life. Have faith in yourself and keep moving forward.

Christine Learmonth

They lied to you, sold you ideas of good and evil, gave you distrust of your body and shame for your prophethood of chaos.

Charles Donaldson

Footnotes for Life

_____

_____

_____

_____

_____

_____

_____

_____

FEBRUARY 20

Paul had been sober for fifteen years and I was acting as if he was still drinking. His kindness was greeted with my recriminations. His gentleness fueled my defensiveness. My anger flared like a fire suddenly out of control provoked by something he did to show he cared. He was trying so hard to make up for lost years and I was thwarting him at every turn. Late one night, I lay awake thinking. As tears rolled onto the pillow, I realized I could never release my anger until I forgave Paul. The more I thought about this, the more free I felt. I was not the judge and jury. I could not continue to judge my husband, only to love and forgive him.

Your pain is the breaking of the shell that encloses your understanding.

Kahlil Gibran

Sallie A. Rodman

Footnotes for Life

_____

_____

_____

_____

_____

_____

_____

FEBRUARY 21

Sound judgment about what is right and what you need to do is based on your system of values. It is only when you are standing on the foundation of your values that you are able to maintain your truth, no matter what the circumstances. The ability to live according to your values, in an unwavering way, depends on how well you have realized your true spiritual identity, and have begun to cultivate that inner state of dignity. The awareness of being God's child allows you to claim your divinity. The awareness of being a student, learning not just from God but also from those around you, of being an example, of becoming a model of whatever you want others to learn, allows you to understand your highest truth and begin to live it.

In your golden heart there is no limit to forgiveness, and no space for disheartenment.

Brahma Kumaris

Brahma Kumaris
World Spiritual University
Footnotes for Life

FEBRUARY 22

Since I had cancer twelve years ago, I have created my own recovery. Every day, I must tend to my body and to my mind. I cannot forget that I am always in recovery. I cannot say to myself, "I do not matter," for I must believe I do. I matter to my family and friends who reach out to me and I to them. I matter to my pets who think there is no person more important in the world. I matter to myself because that is essential to my recovery. To matter. To someone. Somewhere. Every day.

Harriet May Savitz

I long to alleviate the evil, but I cannot. And I too suffer. This has been my life; I found it worth living.

Bertrand Russell

Footnotes for Life

_____

_____

_____

_____

_____

_____

_____

In the stillness of the morning before I get out of bed, I listen for the voice of God and this is what he says, "I give you love, peace and happiness to set you on your way.

I am always watching out for you each and every day.

Do not fear for tomorrow, for today has just begun.

Instead, look for the treasures that come from up above."

Theresa Meehan

I will greet this day with love in my heart. I will love the sun for it warms my bones; yet I will love the rain for it cleanses my spirit.

Og Mandino

Footnotes for Life

_____

_____

_____

_____

_____

_____

_____

_____

My great grandmother had eleven children, washed clothes on a washboard, cooked on a wood-burning stove and lived in a modest shanty with no plumbing or electricity. Although poor by the world's standards, she had riches untold. Her wealth consisted of hope, peace and joy. In my research I discovered Granny Lowe's secrets of success: Live one day at a time, be content with what you have and make someone else happy. These three secrets can change a life from despair into hope, envy to contentment, and sorrow into joy.

Joan Clayton

I want to leave treasures that money can't buy.

Joan Clayton

Footnotes for Life

Somewhere along your path to recovery, God has given you at least one encourager—someone who listens, who is farther along the path than you are, who gives you hope. Is the time right for you to find someone farther back, who needs your encouragement, guidance, a light to see the path? Giving support will energize their recovery . . . and your own.

Joy Neal Kidney

Having chosen our course, without guile and with pure purpose, let us renew our trust in God, and go forward without fear.

Abraham Lincoln

Footnotes for Life

_____

_____

_____

_____

_____

_____

_____

_____

Close your eyes and savor the quiet. Hear the birds chirping, the airplane soaring overhead, the neighborhood moving through its daily rhythm. Listen until the lullaby soothes your spirit and a sense of peace surrounds you. Feel the quiet calm and open the locked window in your heart. You wait, unsure, then your mind quickens when deep, buried hurts stumble out. You're facing the horror again, not wanting to look away anymore. Somehow you survived the abuse all those years ago. The scars are real and will always remain, but today, you realize they don't define you. You're still shaky, but now you feel something like hope. You finally understand it wasn't your fault.

Stress leaves an indelible scar, and the organism pays for its survival after a stressful situation by becoming a little older.

Hans Selye

Joanna Booher

Footnotes for Life

In the midst of a terrible winter storm Tom lay blacked-out on his back in an alley, unaware that drugs and alcohol were about to claim him. Slowly a strange sensation pulled him back. Short, abrasive strokes across his face. His eyes snapped open to find himself nose-to-nose with a pitiful but very large cat. Life soon bottomed-out for Tom but concern for his furry angel gave him the will to hold on. Years later, cradling the old cat, he spoke softly, "You don't have to stay on my account, I'm gonna be okay," and the golden eyes closed for the last time. Companionship and support comes in all shapes and sizes.

John Crusey

No matter how dark things seem to be or actually are, raise your sights and see possibilities—always see them, for they're always there.

Dr. Norman Vincent Peale

Footnotes for Life

_____

_____

_____

_____

_____

_____

_____

_____

What a powerful thing choice is. We can choose to lead and set examples of strength and perseverance, courage and love, or we can give in to our addiction, accept defeat and wallow in a self-pity that will never let go.

We can choose to support those who are strong and in turn lean on them so we no longer have to walk alone. Reflect on your journey and where your path leads. The most difficult choices often lead to the greatest rewards.

Raquel Strand

Destiny is not a matter of chance; it is a matter of choice. It is not a thing to be waited for; it is a thing to be achieved.

William Jennings Bryan

Footnotes for Life

_____

_____

_____

_____

_____

_____

_____

I will not hold onto the memories or the hurtful past, though they are a part of me. I choose to allow them to strengthen me as I move forward. I chose this destiny. I chose this journey. I will begin with my first step, putting one foot steadily in front of the other. Then another. Then another.

Alexandra P.

Let's take the mistakes of the past, and the road-blocking challenges of the present, and build them into stairs that support our climb into the future.

Mattie J. T. Stepanek

Footnotes for Life

_____

_____

_____

_____

_____

_____

_____

_____

Today signals a change in my life. Today, the tide turns me on a new course, a new way of living. Today, I am released of the burdens and pain and suffering that have kept me contained, living small. Today, I am like the vast open ocean, free to flow expansively, surging with powerful energy. As I ebb with my natural life current, an endless horizon of possibilities comes into view. I float through the cool clear waters, refreshed and renewed with hope. The calm waves soothe my spirit and cleanse the sorrow of the past. Today, I glide with the surf, carried gently to a life far bigger than I ever dreamed.

Shary Hauer

Most people live in a very restricted circle of their potential being. We all have reservoirs of energy and genius to draw upon of which we do not dream.

William James

Footnotes for Life

_____

_____

_____

_____

_____

_____

_____

My three-year-old daughter pulled the blankets up under her chin as I tucked her in for the night. "Mommy, does God have arms?"

"No, God is spirit," I replied. "He doesn't have a body like ours."

"Then how does he give hugs?" she asked.

Reaching down to wrap my arms around her in a tight squeeze, I explained, "Whenever God needs arms, he borrows ours."

Emily Chase

What lies behind us and what lies before us are tiny matters compared to what lies within us.

Ralph Waldo Emerson

Footnotes for Life

_____

_____

_____

_____

_____

_____

_____

_____

March 4

I have a busy "committee meeting" in my brain on most days. It's always been there and I have come to accept that it may always be there. However, when I hear too much conversation in my head centered on the idea of "enough-ness," I know it's time to get conscious about those messages. My disease is about "not being enough." It tells me I'm not smart enough, rich enough, pretty enough; the list goes on and on. Once I recognize that line of thinking, I change to a more truthful affirmation—I am enough. I am intelligent enough, I am thin enough, I am simply enough, just the way I am.

Argue for your limitations and sure enough they're yours.

Richard Bach

Anne Conner

Footnotes for Life

_____

_____

_____

_____

_____

_____

_____

At thirty-one I had a doctorate in psychology and had been drinking heavily on and off for fourteen years. My head was so filled with theories and concepts that I thought myself into one blind alley after another. Finally unable to struggle any longer, I shook with fear as I called a friend in recovery. "Charlie, I think I'm an alcoholic. Will you take me to a meeting?" I could feel a comforting, accepting smile beaming out of the telephone. Through the fog of my terror and shame I heard him say, with nearly infinite warmth, "John, I've been waiting a year and a half for you. Of course, I'll take you. It would be an honor."

John C. Friel

Live as if you were to die tomorrow. Learn as if you were to live forever.

Mahatma Gandhi

Footnotes for Life

_____

_____

_____

_____

_____

_____

_____

_____

MARCH 6

When you find yourself trapped, there is only one way out. That way is your trust in a Higher Power.

You do not have to wear yourself out until you are near death. Look around. He may reveal himself to you, just as he revealed himself to me, when I became willing to be carried in loving hands.

David Mead

*Only that day dawns
to which we are awake.*

Henry David Thoreau

Footnotes for Life

_____

_____

_____

_____

_____

_____

_____

Victories often arrive after you have exhausted every ounce of effort and the sweat pours down your face. Sometimes victory is achieved as you stand resolute with feet firmly planted, confronting your enemy face to face.

But there are times when victory is not in the battle at all, but in the understanding that discretion is, indeed, the better part of valor. Whatever shape they come in, celebrate your victories.

Ava Pennington

Just as the body cannot exist without blood, so the soul needs matchless and pure strength of faith.

Mahatma Gandhi

Footnotes for Life

_____

_____

_____

_____

_____

_____

_____

_____

MARCH 8

I honor my own experience and personal truth. I know that no one from my past needs to see things the way I do for me to get better or move on. Trying to convince family members of what I have learned through my own journey can be an exercise in futility and delay my progress. Each of us has our own truth that is unique unto itself. We are all at different levels of understanding and acceptance of who and where we are in life. Each member of my family experienced our childhoods in our own way and have a right to our own perceptions. I do not have to get anyone to see it my way in order for me to feel comfortable. My truth is my truth, theirs is theirs.

If you add to the truth, you subtract from it.

The Talmud

Tian Dayton

Footnotes for Life

Failure. It's one of the most beautiful things in the world. Failure is exciting because it means I'm reaching past what I've always done. It means I'm willing to try new things. It keeps my mind young and energized because the focus isn't on the failure but on the one step closer to a goal to be reached. Goals are reached one failed step at a time.

Glenda Schoonmaker

If you always do what you've always done, then you will always get what you've always gotten.

Unknown

Footnotes for Life

_____

_____

_____

_____

_____

_____

_____

_____

These days my attention is not on fixing others, but on creating a sense of well-being within myself. As I discover new ways of improving the quality of my life I can be sure that I reflect well-being to others. If I am critical of myself, I am quick to condemn and judge others. If my life is full of contradictions, resentments and insecurities, I might be sabotaging the growth of those who come to me seeking help. I must remember that as a helper, I can only be a catalyst for change. In the end, each individual must decide whether or not to embark on a different journey.

Rokelle Lerner

Discovery consists of seeing what everybody has seen and thinking what nobody has thought.

Albert von Szent-Györgyi

Footnotes for Life

_____

_____

_____

_____

_____

_____

_____

I enjoyed fulfilling work as a sign language interpreter until a brain injury left me struggling to re-learn simple tasks. One Sunday, the chair where the interpreter sat for our church service was empty. My heart argued with my bruised brain as I saw the deaf people's disappointment. I knew I had to try. I took my place, looked out into the large congregation and began to panic. But as I looked into the eyes of the deaf congregants my hands took flight. Expressed with the voice in my hands, the words landed lovingly in the hearts and minds of my deaf friends through expectant eyes. In the service of others, I had found and reclaimed my self.

The highest of distinctions is service to others.

King George VI

Jenna Cassell

Footnotes for Life

MARCH 12

Pain of human experiences is universal and a safe setting and a language through which to talk about one's experiences allow people to begin to speak their truth, to own their reality. Ultimately they can put the past behind them, let go of painful familiar scripts and be accountable for their own choices. No one deserves to live a life of fear, pain and shame.

Claudia Black

It is easier to build strong children than to repair broken men.

Frederick Douglas

Footnotes for Life

_____

_____

_____

_____

_____

_____

_____

Just for today, I release all worries.

Just for today, I release all anger.

Just for today, I shall earn my living with integrity.

Just for today, I will be kind to every living thing.

Just for today, I give thanks for all my many blessings.

Reiki Principle

Gratitude makes sense of our past, brings peace for today, and creates a vision for tomorrow.

Melody Beattie

Footnotes for Life

_____

_____

_____

_____

_____

_____

_____

_____

MARCH 14

The gems of real value in our lives are the people who at one time or another have loved us unconditionally. These spiritual guides change from time to time, but what they have in common is their acceptance of us just the way we are. We can keep that love with us today in accepting ourselves as treasured gems. We need to accept ourselves as part of the wealth of the Universe, for without us it would be devoid of the beauty of the human spirit. That beauty is the kind of wealth that provides true happiness. Love is a richness that cannot be devalued.

Yvonne Kaye

If your riches are gems, why don't you take them with you to the other world?

Benjamin Franklin

Footnotes for Life

_____

_____

_____

_____

_____

_____

_____

It is important that we laugh, sing, dance and love. Never stand on the sidelines and be left wondering "what if." Step forward and give life all you have to give. Open doors for others as doors have opened for you. Face the challenges with hope. Meet obstacles with a smile. You never know who may be watching, so be a good example and mentor. Cherish the moments and look to God for answers.

Diane Thompson

God bears with imperfect beings even when they resist His goodness.

Francois de Fenelon

Footnotes for Life

_____

_____

_____

_____

_____

_____

_____

_____

It is one of the most difficult things you can do. And yet, it is very simple, easy and effortless. It is one of the most powerful things you can do. And yet, when you do it you give up the need and the desire for power. What is it? It is letting go of your own ego.

When you can bring yourself to get beyond your own ego, you raise yourself to a whole new level of awareness, experience and effectiveness. When you can think, live and act unconstrained by the limitations of your ego, the possibilities are truly endless. Your worries, your fears, your doubts, anxieties, disappointments and hesitation to move forward are all sustained by your ego. Imagine the power of leaving all those limitations behind.

Flexibility means being able to make problems into teachers.

Brahma Kumaris

Brahma Kumaris
World Spiritual University

Footnotes for Life

_____

_____

_____

_____

_____

_____

_____

_____

My past is no longer here. My present is today. My future is waiting and I will start planning now. I will treat myself with love, make each day a positive one and not allow self-pity to control me.

It is survival of the fittest and I challenge myself to focus not on what others do for me but what I can do with my disorder to help other people.

Stacey Chillemi

Determine that the thing can and shall be done, and then we shall find the way.

Abraham Lincoln

Footnotes for Life

_____

_____

_____

_____

_____

_____

_____

_____

MARCH 18

Vague feelings of discontent or twinges of restlessness are discomforts we have difficulty identifying and they can be disconcerting. Often we are able to handle the obvious problem areas in our recovery but struggle with the subtle pitfalls. Without realizing it, we can choose the wrong things to fill the empty void created by our boredom. It might be as simple as choosing a handful of cookies when a walk would be a better choice. Part of recovery is making wise choices.

Joyce McDonald Hoskins

Expectations are the thief of God's blessings.

Constance K. Hardy

Footnotes for Life

_____

_____

_____

_____

_____

_____

_____

You are enough, you have enough. Everything you need is within you. Maybe for others I believed that, but not myself. I've always felt lacking and wanting. I needed more, something was missing. Should I change jobs? Go back to school? Move? Move on? That "not enough" feeling was always there.

Suddenly, today I understood that "not enough" meant love. That "more" meant love. That thing "missing" was love. Self-love. As I embrace that idea, I recognize and appreciate that I do have enough and I am enough. What a gift to give oneself!

Deb Sellars Karpek

If something is wrong, fix it if you can. But train yourself not to worry. Worry never fixes anything.

Mrs. Ernest Hemingway

Footnotes for Life

_____

_____

_____

_____

_____

_____

_____

_____

MARCH 20

As a teenager I chased after better living through chemicals believing that if you had my troubles, you too would drink and drug. Now that I've learned that most of my troubles came from the drinking and drugging, when I come to a fork in the road I know how to make a sober choice and reap the significant rewards. I remember many nights sitting on a bar stool yakking away about being an artist. Now that I'm in recovery I know how to show up for life and work hard. I am successful. I run my own business. I set goals. I achieve them. I'm not all talk. That's what self-esteem is made of!

Dorri Olds

Nothing is so soothing to our self-esteem as to find our bad traits in our forebears. It seems to absolve us.

Van Wyck Brooks

Footnotes for Life

_____

_____

_____

_____

_____

_____

_____

I spent many years unsuccessfully struggling to change the size and shape of my body. Therein lay the spark for change, the point of departure. The new idea, the only fad I hadn't tried, was to love and accept my body unconditionally at the size and shape I was. This newfound acceptance was the revolutionary act that led me to unprecedented freedom from obsession and dangerous behaviors. My bottom line is I no longer harm myself with food or exercise and I no longer use food or exercise to try to change the size or shape of my body. I've finally come to know beyond a shadow of a doubt that there is nothing wrong with me. Nothing needs to be changed.

It is the mind that makes the body.

Sojourner Truth

Rachel Caplin

Footnotes for Life

MARCH 22

There have been times in my recovery when my life feels dull. That sense of exhilaration and newness isn't present anymore. As a recovering "excitement junkie," I need to practice being comfortable with the stability of a more even existence. Consistency can actually be a comfortable state of being once I get past the old messages about "doing" rather than "being." I can also remember that new and exciting experiences will come my way when it's time. While I'm calmly waiting, I can ask my Higher Power for inspiration and direction on the next chapter of my life.

Anne Conner

Life is a glass given to us to fill; a busy life is filling it with as much as it can hold; a hurried life has had more poured into it than it can contain.

William Adams Brown

Footnotes for Life

_____

_____

_____

_____

_____

_____

_____

Our daughter is an athlete who has run the Chicago and New York marathons. Facing an eight hour surgery for malignant melanoma she related the experience to her hike across the moors in Scotland. "When walking in the driving rain through the barren land, I'd look ahead at the puddles forming. They looked so big and I didn't think I could get across . . . but I did. Every time I got up to the place where I needed to cross, I discovered small pebbles had formed a path for me and each time I've faced a trial, I know God will put the pebbles in place when I need to cross."

Elaine Ingalls Hogg

Courage is the first of human qualities, because it is the quality which guarantees all others.

Winston Churchill

Footnotes for Life

_____

_____

_____

_____

_____

_____

_____

_____

I think that human beings are very imitative creatures; we imitate clothes, hair styles, mannerisms and lifestyles. A man's mind will be influenced by what he listens to and what he reads. And what we think is very important to sobriety.

Today I make an effort to examine my thinking and check it out with a sponsor or in a support group. I know that my dignity in sobriety is connected not only with what I do but also with my attitudes and thoughts. When my thinking begins to go crazy, I know I am in a dangerous place and I need to talk. God created me with the ability to think, therefore, I need to safeguard the information I put in my mind.

Thought makes the whole dignity of man; therefore endeavor to think well, that is the only morality.

Blaise Pascal

Reverend Leo Booth

Footnotes for Life

"Did you notice the beautiful sunrise this morning?" Steven asked. I shook my head no. "Well, I just watched it from my cell and realized how grateful I am that I can see the sunrise through the bars of my window. And, I just had breakfast. My oatmeal wasn't as cold as it often is, which makes it a good day." The sincerity in his voice stopped me in my tracks. Just the day before, Steven learned he would be serving the full term of his DUI sentence, another five years, behind bars. I've never forgotten what I learned from him that beautiful morning. When I start throwing a pity party for myself I remember that I, too, can choose what to focus on in my life.

People become what you encourage them to be, not what you nag them to be.

Scudder N. Parker

Lisa Kugler

Footnotes for Life

MARCH 26

Recovery is a journey from brokenness to wholeness during which we often shut ourselves off from those around us. What we don't readily see is that intentionally alienating ourselves from others is a kind of self-inflicted brokenness. There is no shame in needing others; none of us is complete without human relationships, but if we choose to face life in isolation we will always be deficient in some way.

I would rather define self as the interiorization of community.

James Hillman

At the same time, we must realize that in every relationship we also bring something of value to others that they need in order to be whole. In community, we give and receive strength for the journey.

Lynne Lepley

Footnotes for Life

_____

_____

_____

_____

_____

_____

_____

When going through tragedy to emerge on the other side without having taken on the ugly traits of bitterness, anger and self-pity is no easy task. Hopefully, we come to understand that deep in our souls we are all beautiful. It is this beauty that continues to live on. It's an incredible gift if we can connect with it, not only within ourselves, but also with our loved ones. But just as the ugly duckling was blind to his true being until he saw his reflection, we can't know this truth unless we are willing to look for it. The journey takes courage.

Joyce Harvey

I asked God to give me happiness. God said, "No. I give you blessings. Happiness is up to you."

Unknown

Footnotes for Life

_____

_____

_____

_____

_____

_____

_____

_____

MARCH 28

Today I greet the world, not only with resolutions of what to achieve, but also with a willingness to embrace life as it is. If I miss all that is contained in this moment, then I miss it all. The beauty, purpose and mystery that are always available to me are my real treasures in this world. This year I learn about life and love and simplicity. I want what I pass on to my children to go into their hearts where no one can take it away. I want to know them and I want them to know me.

Tian Dayton

Life was meant to be lived, and curiosity must be kept alive. One must never, for whatever reason, turn his back on life.

Eleanor Roosevelt

Footnotes for Life

_____

_____

_____

_____

_____

_____

_____

Every imaginable form of loss, disappointment or temptation has been experienced countless times and will be repeated as long as man continues to walk the Earth. Pain isn't a new concept but it is experienced fresh in each shattered heart seeking a purpose for life's unpredictable course. Despite our own heartbreaking experiences, we cannot fully comprehend the depth of despair that touches each individual soul. What we can do, is draw from our own experiences a passion to wrap them in tender arms of compassion, cover them with prayer and become, through our own response, a model of God's unconditional love.

Valerie Frost

The finest qualities of our nature can be preserved only by the most delicate handling.

Henry David Thoreau

Footnotes for Life

D ays come and go and the beauty of life is lost when I wander through moments unconsciously. To fully experience life I remind myself of what gave me pleasure as a small child. Sniffing oranges as I peeled the skin. Rolling a caramel around in my mouth. Feeling the swooping thrill as I swished down a slide. Playing with bubbles in a soapy bath. The curiosity and creativity I possessed as a child is still inside of me. All I need to do is remember that my ability to recapture it is there for the taking. I can dance, write, play or listen and in doing so I awaken my senses to celebrate the creative wonderful parts that I possess.

Rokelle Lerner

Some pursue happiness, others create it.

Unknown

Footnotes for Life

_____

_____

_____

_____

_____

_____

_____

_____

It's very early spring; it's still damp and cold. Though the snow has melted off the garden beds, the debris of winter is all that's evident. I stoop down and pull off a bit of matted leaves here and there, pull back the few branches of evergreen left over from the holidays, and I'm amazed to see the little shoots of bulbs and perennials clearly showing above the soil. I am always reminded that, each spring the new shoots in the garden return and soon blossom into flowers. I also remember that I too experience new growth all the time, especially after I clear the debris of what's no longer needed in my life.

Anne Conner

Criticism, like rain, should be gentle enough to nourish a man's growth without destroying his roots.

Frank A. Clark

Footnotes for Life

_____

_____

_____

_____

_____

_____

_____

_____

READER/CUSTOMER CARE SURVEY

HEMG

We care about your opinions! Please take a moment to fill out our online Reader Survey at
http://survey.hcibooks.com. As a **"THANK YOU"** you will receive a **VALUABLE INSTANT COUPON** towards future
book purchases as well as a **SPECIAL GIFT** available only online! Or, you may mail this card back to us
and we will send you a copy of our exciting catalog with your valuable coupon inside.

First Name _____ MI. _____ Last Name _____

Address _____ Email _____

State _____ Zip _____ City _____

1. Gender	4. Annual Household Income	6. Marital Status	Comments
☐ Female ☐ Male	☐ under $25,000	☐ Single	
2. Age	☐ $25,000 - $34,999	☐ Married	
☐ 8 or younger	☐ $35,000 - $49,999	☐ Divorced	
☐ 9-12 ☐ 13-16	☐ $50,000 - $74,999	☐ Widowed	
☐ 17-20 ☐ 21-30	☐ over $75,000		
☐ 31+			
3. Did you receive this book as a gift?	**5. What are the ages of the children living in your house?**		
☐ Yes ☐ No	☐ 0 - 14 ☐ 15+		

BUSINESS REPLY MAIL

FIRST-CLASS MAIL PERMIT NO 45 DEERFIELD BEACH, FL

POSTAGE WILL BE PAID BY ADDRESSEE

Health Communications, Inc.

3201 SW 15th Street

Deerfield Beach FL 33442-9875

I just celebrated my first Dry Decade. At my first A.A. meeting, I cried. I couldn't speak and I went home and finished off my bottle of vodka. But I went back the next day. So how were the first ten years? It was heavy on the major life stuff; I got married, quit my job, had two babies. How I did it all without my Stoli, I don't know. But I couldn't have done it with my Stoli, either. Ten years is a long time, but then not. To see where I've been and where I am now is both confusing and clear. It's ten years that I may not have lived to see, had I continued sailing into darkness.

Julia Jergensen Edelman

When walking through the "valley of shadows," remember, a shadow is cast by a light.

H.K. Barclay

Footnotes for Life

_____

_____

_____

_____

_____

_____

_____

_____

APRIL 2

Early on you may find obstacles in your path and have the constant feeling of being unfit. Sometimes you blame yourself for the nagging weakness that causes you to regress. Re-adjust your thinking; take the pressure off and stop beating yourself up. Shame and guilt may flood you no matter how great your willpower is. Write down your trigger points. Replace these negative thoughts with positive ones. Conquer this internal battle by summoning your inner strength and purpose.

Suzanne Baginskie

He can inspire a group only if he himself is filled with confidence and hope of success.

Floyd V. Filson

Footnotes for Life

_____

_____

_____

_____

_____

_____

_____

Serenity is an expression of my spiritual nature and—much as I might try—I cannot experience it through hard work and determination. Instead, I must learn to let go of my anger, resentments, demands and the need to be "right."

Then and only then will I be at peace with myself and the world around me.

Jeff McFarland

> *Nothing can bring you peace but yourself.*
> Ralph Waldo Emerson

Footnotes for Life

_____

_____

_____

_____

_____

_____

_____

_____

APRIL 4

Timing is everything. When is it time for me to make decisions about my recovery? When will I no longer wait to do something about my family situation, my pain or my destructive relationships? I know that postponing help will only allow my problems to continue. I have been waiting for the "right time" to start acting for my benefit when in fact, there is no better time than now. Today I will take care of myself. I will wait no longer for the help I need. The "right time" has come.

Rokelle Lerner

Let your life lightly dance on the edges of Time like dew on the tip of a leaf.

Tagore

Footnotes for Life

_____

_____

_____

_____

_____

_____

_____

Were we given the choice, not many of us would choose to learn the hard lessons. They overtake us nevertheless. And yet they are not without value, these painful experiences. Whether visited upon us unfairly at the hand of another or brought on by our own bad choices, we have the ability to select our attitude from this point forward. We can glean every possible goodness from present circumstances and resolve to learn all that may be learned, not only for our own benefit but to help ease the way of fellow learners.

Experience: that most brutal of teachers. But you learn, my God do you learn.

C.S. Lewis

Rhonda Brunea

Footnotes for Life

_____

_____

_____

_____

_____

_____

_____

_____

Marathons are won one inch at a time, and twenty pounds are lost one ounce at a time. We must simply repeat the same action over and over and over again, until we win. We only get what we are working for by a series of little actions, one boring move at a time. Success in life has to do with a simple faithfulness to do what we know how to do, one task at a time, one moment at a time. Success has everything to do with simply waking up one more day and moving forward.

Barbara A. Croce

Big shots are only little shots who keep shooting.

Christopher Morley

Footnotes for Life

_____

_____

_____

_____

_____

_____

_____

Sometimes I'm more generous and forgiving towards others than of myself. It's easy to be at war within—harsh, judgmental, focusing on faults. Today will be the beginning of fairness. I'll be a friend to myself; generous and forgiving. I will talk gently, and appreciate my strengths. I acknowledge there are areas of needed improvement that I must work on, but I will practice being as supportive with my inner person as I am to others. This is especially critical for my recovery. I can be my own best friend in word, thought and deed.

Brenda Nixon

Things which matter most must never be at the mercy of things which matter least.

Goethe

Footnotes for Life

_____

_____

_____

_____

_____

_____

_____

_____

APRIL 8

If we all approached each of our days as if they were the last, perhaps we would finally understand that a life well lived is our greatest responsibility and our ultimate glory. The prospect of death wouldn't be so frightening. Of course we are a relentlessly hopeful group—that's what makes us human—and who are we not to believe we can live forever? In many ways we do.

*And if the earthly
no longer knows
your name, whisper to
the silent earth:
I'm flowing. To the
flashing water say:
I am.*

Rainer Maria Rilke

Take the time to savor, like never before, every rise and set of the sun, every phase of every moon, each rain shower and cloudless sky, all the rich and myriad sights and sounds and smells that are ordinary and extraordinary.

Nancy Burke

Footnotes for Life

_____

_____

_____

_____

_____

_____

_____

What do you say to someone who has manipulated, abused and controlled you for years? What do you say to someone who has lied to you for your entire life? What do you say to someone who ultimately wants to destroy you? I sat in silence for what seemed like an eternity. Finally I asked, "Why do you try to control my every move? Why won't you just leave me alone?" In the few seconds that it took me to ask those two questions, I felt just a little bit of separation from ED—an acronym for my eating disorder. And it felt so good.

No one can make you feel inferior without your consent.

Eleanor Roosevelt

Jenni Schaefer

Footnotes for Life

_____

_____

_____

_____

_____

_____

_____

_____

I often feel so impatient when things don't change more quickly than I want them to. My old way of thinking left me desperate for immediate gratification. If something didn't happen right away, I changed course and tried another approach with the same high standards of immediacy. That included everything from what I cooked for dinner, to the new position for which I applied, to demanding that a relationship develop the way I wanted it to, rather than waiting to see how it would develop naturally. Today, I have learned to be conscious of slowing down, lowering my expectations and understanding the different stages in any process. I am happier all around, and I cook better meals!

Growth in wisdom may be exactly measured by decrease in bitterness.

Friedrich Nietzsche

Anne Conner

Footnotes for Life

How do I put the pieces of my life back together? What do I do with those mis-shapen parts of myself, the parts that are old, frayed and tattered? Let me take a lesson from the quilt maker. I will examine all parts of myself before I make decisions to "keep" or "throw out." Who I am is all I have to work with. There is no need to rip myself apart and start over. Recovery is the art of making order out of chaos. With love and patience, I am learning how to make order out of my personal chaos. A work of art is in the making.

You must understand the whole of life, not just one little part of it.

J. Krishnamurti

Rokelle Lerner

Footnotes for Life

_____

_____

_____

_____

_____

_____

_____

_____

Thanking God for a specific attribute brings him into your everyday life and reminds you he has an answer for your every need. On a day you feel disorganized, or frustrated with someone else's disorganization, thank him for being organized. When you feel misunderstood, thank him for being understanding. When you experience his perfect timing that turned out to be different from yours, thank him for being timely. Thank him for being generous on a day you are experiencing his unmerited abundance. Thank him for being a forgiver, on a day you need forgiveness, or need him to help you forgive. When you feel less important than others, thank him for being interested in all of us.

The strength of a man's virtue must not be measured by his efforts, but by his ordinary life.

Blaise Pascal

Lana Fletcher

Footnotes for Life

_____

_____

_____

_____

_____

_____

_____

There is something unique about each one of us. We all have different ways of expressing ourselves, of handling adversity or conflict. Misunderstandings are the basis for most quarrels and it requires patience to listen to what is said between the lines. To recover from hurts and injustices I must first look at myself. If something I did or said added to the conflict, then I must take responsibility for my actions and apologize. If the other person cannot accept it and the relationship suffers, it is their problem. I have done my best.

Joan Clayton

> *Forgiveness is the bridge for restoring relationships.*
>
> Joan Clayton

Footnotes for Life

_____

_____

_____

_____

_____

_____

_____

_____

APRIL 14

I t is a sign of wisdom to be able to set goals and then, having done so, to let them go. All that is required for success is a vision of the destination. The journey itself will reveal the means that will take you there.

Mistakes will not throw you off course unless you let them stop you. A good navigator keeps a sure eye on the final destination, but steers there through a series of approximations.

Brahma Kumaris World Spiritual University

Your determination pulls success toward you, and your focus pushes obstacles away.

Brahma Kumaris

Footnotes for Life

We can be so quick to judge, to label actions, people, circumstance as good or bad, right or wrong. By doing so we essentially limit our experience of life. Even the painful path of an alcoholic need not be labeled or judged as bad, for this path provides perspective, consciousness, gifts unattainable in any other way.

Today, I let go of my need to label or judge, remembering that often gifts are well disguised, and that God has a much bigger perspective than I.

Jeffrey R. Anderson

Don't judge each day by the harvest you reap, but by the seeds you plant.

Robert Louis Stevenson

Footnotes for Life

_____

_____

_____

_____

_____

_____

_____

_____

I love to awaken to the birdsong outside my bedroom window as I wonder what the new day will bring. As I look outside, it looks cold and damp as if it has been raining. Yet, regardless of the weather, the little robin perched on her branch will continue singing. The robin knows that all her needs will be provided for daily. There is no need to worry.

> *Life is really simple, but men insist on making it complicated.*
> Confucius

I also have needs, but unlike the little robin, I do worry. But, just for this morning, I will surrender my cares to the one God who provides for all creation.

Theresa Meehan

Footnotes for Life

_____

_____

_____

_____

_____

_____

_____

APRIL 17

For me, the greatest part of recovery is the feeling that I am never alone. I have a whole sober community that I share my life with. One day someone is holding me up; another day that same person is shaky and I get to be their strong support. In recovery I have been given so much love and so much hope. A passage in "Promises" from *The Big Book of Alcoholics Anonymous* says it best, "We are going to know a new freedom and a new happiness. No matter how far down the scale we have gone, we will see how our experience can benefit others."

I once was lost but now I'm found.

John Newton

Dorri Olds

Footnotes for Life

_____

_____

_____

_____

_____

_____

_____

_____

APRIL 18

Choosing an attitude of joy regardless of circumstances is a courageous act of faith, but it is also a matter of will. Such an attitude enables us to set a strong hand to whatever good we can do, lighting brave little candles against the darkness. It is a conscious decision to make my world better rather than worse. I choose this day to notice and savor every good thing. I will walk in joy that cannot be disturbed by the actions of others, but can be passed on to those who desire it.

Rhonda Brunea

We cannot cure the world of sorrows, but we can choose to live in joy.

Joseph Campbell

Footnotes for Life

_____

_____

_____

_____

_____

_____

_____

_____

Paint it all. Not just the sunshine and the rainbows, but also the floods and the storms. Write it all. Not just about laughter and cheers, celebrations and victories, but also write about pains and tears, failures and fears. Because as the years go by and you go over your life, you will not want to miss out on anything. For even the faintest smile, even the smallest teardrop has made your life as it is.

Maria Isabel A. Arellano

Imagination disposes of everything; it creates beauty, justice, happiness, which is everything in the world.

Blaise Pascal

Footnotes for Life

_____

_____

_____

_____

_____

_____

_____

_____

APRIL 20

I accept that each time I grow or change, somewhere pain will be present. Issues that I may have accumulated over a period of decades I am dealing with in a much shorter time frame. The pain of confronting myself in these ways will be present alongside the joy that I feel. The easiest way to have the joy rests in not denying the pain, which is also a natural part of the process. All change requires a giving up, and this in itself is cause for mourning. It is this giving up, however, that clears the path for change. I know today that I am going through a purification process and though it is not easy, it is deeply worthwhile.

Tian Dayton

In order to unify ourselves we must change, renounce, give ourselves; and this violence to ourselves partakes of pain.

Pierre Teilhard de Chardin

Footnotes for Life

_____

_____

_____

_____

_____

_____

_____

When our last child left home I had "empty nest" syndrome big time. "Let's get in the pickup and go for a drive," my husband said, brushing away my tears. After a few miles I saw it. A large piece of gnarled white driftwood had been discarded by a country road. The white wood glistened in the sunlight. We put this treasure in our front yard. After many years it still stands, sharing its beauty while reminding me the best things in life are free. Letting go of my children was hard, but like my driftwood, they glisten with beauty in their freedom too.

Joan Clayton

It takes a lot of courage to release the familiar and seemingly secure, to embrace the new.

Alan Cohen

Footnotes for Life

_____

_____

_____

_____

_____

_____

_____

_____

How many times did our mother talk to us about keys? The key to happiness was trust. The key to a decent meal was practice. Being prepared was the key to end all keys. Save three months' pay (in case you lose your job). Keep a canned ham in the pantry (for unexpected company). Have clean underwear (in case you have to go to the hospital). But I wasn't prepared for her to die. I wasn't prepared for a tomorrow without her. Not until our four-year-old granddaughter Amy leaned over Mom's coffin and shook her sleeve and whispered, "When you get to Heaven, say hello to my other grandma, okay?" A child passed us the key.

Mary Lee Moynan

To live fully is to let go and die with each passing moment, and to be reborn in each new one.

Jack Kornfield

Footnotes for Life

_____

_____

_____

_____

_____

_____

_____

_____

L ife is fair because everything balances out; tears are eventually replaced with laughter, loneliness with companionship, fear with bravery, and pain with strength.

Today I embrace this adventure called life—taking it all in. I am able to accept what comes my way even if it's a deep valley because I know there's a mountaintop to come.

Brenda Nixon

Life is not so much a matter of position as of disposition.

Ralph Waldo Emerson

Footnotes for Life

_____

_____

_____

_____

_____

_____

_____

_____

Glimpses of divine guidance do not usually appear to me as flashes of inspiration or overwhelming feelings of spiritual bliss. Often they arrive more subtly, as in a magazine article someone sends to me, or a book I happen to pick up without knowing why. I find my answers in the everyday moments as often as I do in the breathtaking cathedrals or quiet times of prayer. When I am too busy looking for the grand gesture, I often miss the soft whisper. Today I will keep my mind open to the tiny messages that appear to me throughout the day. I have faith that they are there; it is up to me to be open to receiving them.

Amy Ellis

Start by doing what is necessary then do what is possible. And suddenly, you are doing the impossible.

St. Francis of Assisi

Footnotes for Life

_____

_____

_____

_____

_____

_____

_____

We often grasp the stem of a rose precariously, fearing the pain of getting pricked. Just as sometimes, in a difficult situation, we tend to dance around the real problem in hopes of not getting hurt. We make excuses for unseemly actions committed by a loved one or ourselves. We refuse to discuss an issue that may force us to change our familiar lifestyle. We convince ourselves that a difficult task is probably not necessary after all. In avoiding the problem we lose the opportunity to correct it. We remain fearful and out of control. The fact is that by grasping the stem of a rose firmly one does not feel the prick of the thorns.

Only by facing fears can we defuse them and put ourselves back in control.

Hugh Delehanty

Kay Conner Pliszka

Footnotes for Life

_____

_____

_____

_____

_____

_____

_____

_____

Before recovery, we had many questions, the most frequent being "Why me?" Our answers to that were often too painful to face, so we drowned ourselves in alcohol, substances, food or sex.

The morning after, there still were no answers. Just for today, we'll ask: "Why not me?"

Candy Killion

What is the answer? In that case, what is the question?

Gertrude Stein

Footnotes for Life

_____

_____

_____

_____

_____

_____

_____

_____

Everything you need has already been given to you. You have legs so you can turn and face your fears. You have arms to reach out to others. You have shoulders to brace yourself when bad times come. You have ears so you can hear the advice of others. You have eyes to see what needs to be done. And you have a smile so you can always show the face in the mirror that you're going to be okay.

Shelley Wake

Be gentle with yourself, learn to love yourself, to forgive yourself, for only as we have the right attitude toward ourselves can we have the right attitude toward others.

Wilfred Peterson

Footnotes for Life

_____

_____

_____

_____

_____

_____

_____

_____

As I become healthier, my desire to live joyfully grows. Healing means that I no longer want to live in fear, indecision or despair. If this means that I must leave a painful or destructive situation, I am free to do so. No longer do I believe that I am supposed to suffer, nor do I believe that God is ready to punish me at any moment. These beliefs are part of the addicted family sickness. Getting well means acknowledging God's love and knowing that my healing is an expression of my Higher Power. I am making daily choices to avoid beliefs or feelings that throw me back into self-defeating cycles. I am living my life based upon the firm belief that I deserve to find joy and happiness.

*Believe that life is worth living and
your belief will help create the fact.*

William James

Rokelle Lerner

Footnotes for Life

Believe in yourself, it is your most valuable commodity. This inner spiritual inspiration will help you find the strength to commit yourself for the long-term healing process. Your acceptance will cultivate character and patience. Denial will soon pass. As you reach for your goal the reality will overcome your old desires. A wealth of happiness erases your stress of yesterday while creating a strong accountable bond for today. Your protective covering will yield to the richness that life's new pathway will bring; the need for a sense of personal fulfillment and satisfaction.

Suzanne Baginskie

While it takes courage to achieve greatness, it takes more courage to find fulfillment in being ordinary.

Marilyn Thomsen

Footnotes for Life

D arkness is relentless in conquering everything in its path with negativity and hopelessness. "All is lost," cries out its hapless victim. Then the dawn quietly breaks through, gently overpowering its opponent.

The exhausted soul is re-energized and consumed with thoughts of endless possibilities, hopes and dreams. A new life is born and the dawn is victorious. Darkness retreats with wounded spirit, mourning its loss and wondering how the gentleness of dawn can be so effective.

Expect the dawn of a new beginning in the dark nights of life.

Lloyd John Ogilvie

Irma Newland

Footnotes for Life

I work with children who have been ravaged by tragedy and abuse. Most days I am simply amazed and proud that these kids, especially with their acting out and "behavior problems," have survived. One little girl in particular had been victimized at every turn in her young life. During our initial session I was given all the proof I needed of a child's resilience as she serenaded me with the best rendition of "Itsy Bitsy Spider" I've ever heard. Her ability to do that reminded me that despite the awful things I see every day, mine is a great reward to meet just one of these kids, who no matter what happens in their life, can still sing.

Those who wish to sing, always find a song.

Swedish Proverb

Jennifer M. Reinsch

Footnotes for Life

_____

_____

_____

_____

_____

_____

_____

_____

MAY 2

Spring arrives. The start of the new season inspires you to begin anew. You climb another step in your healing progress, an acceptance of a stronger you. The snow melts away like the anxious feelings you've finally shed. The ice turns into cool water and with it your worries trickle away. Your head and heart yield to the warm gentle breeze. The challenges that threatened you are easier to overcome. Life becomes simpler and each day brighter as hope and faith prevail.

Suzanne Baginskie

If the simple things of nature have a message that you understand, rejoice, for your soul is alive.

Eleonora Duse

Footnotes for Life

_____

_____

_____

_____

_____

_____

_____

I have something now that I did not have as a child in an alcoholic home. I have choices. It wasn't always like that. For example, we had the same thing for dinner every night — 365 days a year! What we had for dinner was tension because no one wanted to be there. I am an adult and a father now. If I don't learn new ways, if I don't learn healthy behaviors and if I am not recovering, not only would it affect our children, but someday I could sit at a dinner table with grandchildren who learned to hate dinner. Family rituals are passed from generation to generation. Recovering shows us how to change them.

Robert J. Ackerman

I will be an adult child of an alcoholic until the day I die, but I am not going to die one more day because I am an adult child of an alcoholic.

Robert J. Ackerman

Footnotes for Life

_____

_____

_____

_____

_____

_____

_____

_____

MAY 4

We may have become so accustomed to hardship and pain that we have lost our ability to recognize a good thing when it arrives. We have become preoccupied looking out for the next disaster that will somehow need to be handled. When better times arrive, many of us feel like imposters, undeserving of such favor. We must remember that simply because life has been a certain way in the past does not require it always to be so. We can train our hearts to recognize and accept the good. We do ourselves a great kindness in learning to gratefully accept positive, life-giving occurrences as easily as we once accepted gloom.

Rhonda Brunea

Nothing is too wonderful to be true.

Michael Faraday

Footnotes for Life

_____

_____

_____

_____

_____

_____

_____

_____

I f you want to change your behavior, focus on the thinking which causes it. Thoughts are like seeds. From them grow your attitudes and, in turn, your actions.

When you build a house, every brick counts. When you build character, every thought counts. So think constructively.

Brahma Kumaris
World Spiritual University

It is because you are determined, not flawless, that you attain perfection.

Brahma Kumaris

Footnotes for Life

_____

_____

_____

_____

_____

_____

_____

_____

MAY 6

Another rainy day—and I was so hoping for some bright sunshine. At first I feel disappointed, but then I begin to realize how comfy and cozy I feel inside my home curled up in a throw with a good book. I listen to the soft patter of drops outside my window, and I think I can feel the Earth soaking up and drinking in the nourishing rain. I imagine seeing the roots of my perennials and vegetables; fat and juicy from the moisture they are taking in. I think about how relaxed and refreshed I now feel, having been gifted with a day of repose. What joy—another rainy day.

Anne Conner

You have to accept whatever comes, and the only important thing is that you meet it with courage and with the best that you have to give.

Eleanor Roosevelt

Footnotes for Life

_____

_____

_____

_____

_____

_____

_____

My mother had a stroke that left her struggling to talk, walk and swallow. She had no trouble hearing. We spoke of love. We told her our secrets. Then, one night, we put Mom in a wheelchair and took her to church for a service for the sick. The place was packed. "Raise your hand," said the priest, "if you think your illness is a punishment from God." I watched in disbelief as my good mother slowly lifted her hand just inches off her lap. That's when I learned that healing begins in the heart. In time, Mom walked and talked again. Trust God with your secrets.

Mary Lee Moynan

True friendship is like sound health; the value of it is seldom known until it is lost.

Charles Caleb Colton

Footnotes for Life

_____

_____

_____

_____

_____

_____

_____

_____

MAY 8

I was a freshman in college, three hours from home and not one face at the meeting looked familiar. During a lecture the mention of "Al-Anon" had caught my attention. That was a new one on me. No harm in checking it out—for clinical research reasons, of course.

I looked for a seat way in the back and began having second thoughts when someone touched my arm. "Please, join us." I didn't know what to do, or if I belonged there. I felt eyes searching, looking for clues, trying to uncover my secrets, my memory. In a moment of true clarity, as I tried desperately to come up with an excuse for leaving, the woman simply said, "It's okay—we know."

*Love wholeheartedly,
be surprised, give
thanks and praise—
then you will discover
the fullness of your life.*

Brother David Steindl-Rast

Patricia Holdsworth

Footnotes for Life

MAY 9

There is a great deal of power in humility. Sometimes that power is useful for your own protection. Sometimes it is useful in the protection of others. The power of humility allows you to see the benefit in everything, even the criticisms of others. It enables you to say, "Maybe there's something for me to learn here. Someone is saying this to me, there must be something to it." Your own self-respect works to keep you steady, no matter what comes your way.

Brahma Kumaris
World Spiritual University

Dive deeply into life's mysteries, and fly high above life's challenges, all the while keeping your feet firmly on the ground.

Brahma Kumaris

Footnotes for Life

_____

_____

_____

_____

_____

_____

_____

_____

MAY 10

This morning I wake up looking forward to what I can accomplish. I have chosen my path and I will concentrate on positive goals; the power of ambition and embracing change. I will embody positive transformation and revel in every step I take in the process of becoming who I want to be, moving forward with determination toward my future.

Intelligence without ambition is a bird without wings.

C. Archie Danielson

Stacey Chillemi

Footnotes for Life

_____

_____

_____

_____

_____

_____

_____

It may be impossible to capture life in all of its beauty, splendor and glory. Yet, by catching even bits and pieces of those significant moments, we are endowed with the wonderful opportunity to relive them, to savor them once more. And then we realize life is truly beautiful.

Maria Isabel A. Arellano

Some people have a wonderful capacity to appreciate again and again, freshly and naively, the basic goods of life, with awe, pleasure, wonder, and even ecstasy.

A.H. Maslow

Footnotes for Life

_____

_____

_____

_____

_____

_____

_____

_____

MAY 12

I was used to living with insanity. Living with an alcoholic parent prepared me for survival. I learned to enter into destructive relationships and then to wait for the craziness to end. I learned to see a person not for who they are, but for whom they might become . . . if only. I now know I must protect myself emotionally. It's not safe to place my psyche in the hands of an insane person. I was not put on this Earth to be abused emotionally or physically. I cannot wait for permission to get help or leave an abusive relationship. I cannot wait for overwhelming approval from others for my choices. My life is my own and I must make decisions in my own best interest.

Rokelle Lerner

Footnotes for Life

> *I cannot think of any need in childhood as strong as the need for a father's protection.*
>
> Sigmund Freud

Leave the whispers of the tempter. Today, the strength to walk away is within reach. The taste still charms, but the enemy lives there. An image of new life clings to the mirror. The sweetness of sin turns to bitter memory. Once held captive by cravings, release comes through prayer. Life's path was steep, but now grows level. Peace replaces the agony of physical yearnings. A fortress shields me from the tempter. Tomorrow, fill my heart with more prayers to protect me.

Ann Coogler

Trials, temptations, disappointments—all these are helps instead of hindrances, if one uses them rightly.

James Buckham

Footnotes for Life

_____

_____

_____

_____

_____

_____

_____

_____

I can think of no burden that can be heavier upon the shoulders and conscience of someone than the wreckage of one's past, left untended.

The Steps give us the tools to relieve ourselves of that burden, clean up the wreckage and live happy, joyous and free with the freedom, excitement and wonder of a child once again.

Jeffrey R. Anderson

Pain nourishes courage. You can't be brave if you've only had wonderful things happen to you.

Mary Tyler Moore

Footnotes for Life

_____

_____

_____

_____

_____

_____

_____

_____

Astudy of people living over one-hundred years included their secret of happy living. They awakened each day being grateful for another day of life, stating life was too short to hold grudges or spend time complaining. Every day presents an opportunity to be happy. Joy is obtained by making others happy. All it takes is a little act of kindness . . . a note, a smile, an encouraging word, a pat on the back and a loving heart.

We can learn a lot from these centenarians. The gift of life is priceless.

Being happy today takes care of tomorrow!

Joan Clayton

Joan Clayton

Footnotes for Life

_____

_____

_____

_____

_____

_____

_____

_____

MAY 16

Hardships sensitize us to the everyday parts of life. When we have been stripped bare by the happenings of a dark season, the simple fragrance of lilac on a spring evening, the smile of a stranger, or even the pleasure of crunching a carrot can wrap themselves around us like a hug.

These ordinary events are like a cool drink of water in a parched land; we can take them in and allow them to flood the dry places in us.

Barbara A. Croce

Take the most difficult challenge you are now facing and turn it into the greatest opportunity to grow simply by changing how you see it. Dead ends then become turning points.

Bob Perks

Footnotes for Life

When I get a very strong intuitive message, I will listen to it. I may not be right but I will not discount the feeling or the impulse, knowing that intuition plays an important part in my life. My intuition is real. It is a combination of feelings and instincts that help me to navigate this world. I will not silence that quiet inner voice with "shoulds" today. Living true to my insides is more comfortable for me than working around them. Intuition is real. It is there to guide me.

Tian Dayton

Lead me from the unreal to the real.
Lead me from darkness to light.
Lead me from death to immortality.

Brihadaranyaka Upanishad

Footnotes for Life

_____

_____

_____

_____

_____

_____

_____

_____

MAY 18

Life is full of choices that we make with great and little thought. Whatever the case, you should look back on the moment without regret. Regret is empty and futile and brings with it stagnation. Instead look forward with wishes. Wishes of another opportunity to make another choice with the memory of the lesson learned from that outcome.

Michelle Gipson

I have no regrets, only many, many wishes!

Michelle Gipson

Footnotes for Life

_____

_____

_____

_____

_____

_____

_____

I run the risk of getting burned out when I give wholly to others that which I need myself. When I see to it that my own needs are met, I am not tempted to fill my unmet needs in ways that harm others and myself. I seek nurturing support from my friends and my Higher Power and take time to relax and unwind. I understand that if I fail to support myself I become exhausted, lethargic and angry, helping no one at all. Attending to my own needs before I help someone else is an act of love.

Rokelle Lerner

Hope is faith in the me yet to be.

Treatment Counselor

Footnotes for Life

_____

_____

_____

_____

_____

_____

_____

_____

MAY 20

We never knew each other, let alone had a relationship as sisters. She was the first daughter of my dad, but we had different mothers. Our father had fallen in love with one of his students, a girl fifteen years his junior. He left his wife and young daughter and married the student, who became my mother. We had lived separate lives, become women, wives and mothers, coming together as our father lay dying. I was impressed with her courage and her talents and I admired her forgiving spirit toward a father who had abandoned her. We heal because of the pain we share and in doing so, refuse to repeat the mistakes of our parents.

You can't shake hands with a clenched fist.

Indira Gandhi

Miriam Hill

Footnotes for Life

Life is like soup. The same ingredients will taste differently tomorrow than today and the process is quite different experienced alone, or with another.

Two people can use the same recipe; yet end up with a different flavor and every person will have a unique experience of the same ingredients.

You don't have to know what is in it to like it and of course, there is no one right way to do it.

Creating it with love makes all the difference.

Jeffrey R. Anderson

All life is an experiment. The more experiments you make the better.

Ralph Waldo Emerson

Footnotes for Life

Someone once asked me how to pray. I think prayer is a bit like sex. It's what happens between consenting people. So here's how it works for me. I talk. God listens. So you might ask "How do you know God listens?" That's the tricky part. One time, I turned a picture on its side and decided that if God's answer to my plea was "yes" then in the morning, the picture would be straight. Well that didn't work. But strangely enough, God's answer was yes. Twenty-four hours later, I met the man I would marry. At our wedding, my best friend gave us a plaque "God gives the best to those who leave the choice to him."

Mary Lee Moynan

When you have laboriously accomplished your daily task, go to sleep in peace. God is awake.

Victor Hugo

Footnotes for Life

_____

_____

_____

_____

_____

_____

_____

_____

My friend was showing me his early spring vegetable garden and he said, "And here is where the kale is coming up." I looked down and all I saw was dry dirt. "You mean, where the kale will soon come up?" "No, look," he said, "It's up already." I squatted down to look more closely and still only saw small stones and dusty soil. "Look," he said, "Right here." And there they were, as clear as bright green seedlings against dark, sandy soil. Suddenly, I could see fifty of them all in a row where I had seen nothing moments before. Sometimes, we need another pair of eyes to help us see what's right in front of us.

Gratitude unlocks the fullness of life. It turns denial into acceptance, chaos to order, confusion to clarity.

Melody Beattie

Anne Conner

Footnotes for Life

_____

_____

_____

_____

_____

_____

_____

_____

His brief but tormented young life was punctuated by recurring visits to the ER for treatment of unexplained, questionable injuries too numerous to count. The responsible adults who were supposed to be providing love couldn't control their own anger, impulses and frustrations. He shouldn't have been allowed to slip through the cracks, but in this imperfect world, he did. The battered, wounded youngster experienced moments of comfort and safety as he passed into the next life surrounded by the love that he so desperately needed and deserved in this life. Be a source of love and comfort to someone every day.

The hunger for love is much more difficult to remove than the hunger for bread.

Mother Teresa

Laura Hayes Lagana

Footnotes for Life

I was the daughter with "so much potential" as my mother used to say. I used the potential to hide my drug habit, living a lie, dreading the day anyone discovered my awful secret. That was over seven years ago. My family's love and encouragement never wavered and today I am fully enmeshed in my family. I belong. I have a wonderful job, and I'm active in my church and community. My relationship with my fourteen-year-old son is incredible. I am there to guide him, love him and to be a light in his world. So, once again my mom was right . . . I do have potential. And every day in my recovery, I live it.

If you can't be a good example, then you'll just have to be a horrible warning.

Catherine Aird

Tracey W. Lee

Footnotes for Life

_____

_____

_____

_____

_____

_____

_____

_____

MAY 26

The words "Here I go again" indicate tears are on the way when I talk about something near and dear to my heart; like helping a youth from a broken home. For years I didn't express deep-seated emotional thoughts to avoid the pain and embarrassment of losing control, of crying. Finally I realized the benefit of expressing my true feelings. I changed.

The more often a man feels without acting, the less he'll be able to act. And in the long run, the less he'll be able to feel.

C.S. Lewis

Now I cry from strength and courage, not from weakness and fright. Now I express my deep thoughts. If I cry, others hopefully will see the value in my tears. Just maybe they will see the value in their tears also.

George H. Moffett

Footnotes for Life

_____

_____

_____

_____

_____

_____

_____

When Faith announced, "I have chosen the song for the father and daughter dance at my wedding," Mina was shocked. Faith's father was disabled and dependent on his scooter, but Faith was insistent they would have this dance. The night of the wedding the band began to play Faith's song as Mina prayed for a miracle. Faith hugged her dad and grasped the handles of his scooter. They slowly circled the floor; mindless of the teary-eyed crowd. A determined Faith fulfilled her dream and Mina learned a valuable lesson. Nothing is impossible if one is committed to her dream.

Any man can be a father but it takes someone special to be a dad.

Anne Geddes

Myrna Beth Lambert

Footnotes for Life

MAY 28

My life is a symphony that I create. I can make it beautiful and soothing to the ear or strident and cacophonous. Focusing on losses and disappointments brings discordant notes into play. My soul cramps and I can no longer find the air to breathe a clear note through my instrument. When I instead turn to regard the good with a thankful heart, tragedy transforms into glory, disappointment becomes opportunity, and discord melts into harmony. The music of my life encourages listening hearts to rest and heal, even while bringing restoration to me.

Rhonda Brunea

You know, sometimes it is the artist's task to find out how much music you can still make with what you have left.

Itzhak Perlman

Footnotes for Life

Today is today. Today is not yesterday, crushing you with the mistakes you have made. Today is not tomorrow, which is always out of your grasp. But you can take hold of today.

You can face it. You can deal with it. You can rejoice in the gift that it is.

Unwrap this present with the awe of a five-year-old on Christmas morning. Pull off the bow, rip the wrapping paper and give thanks to him who provided you this gift today.

Sharon Siepel

Do not pray for easy lives. Pray to be stronger. Do not pray for tasks equal to your powers. Pray for powers equal to your tasks.

Phillips Brooks

Footnotes for Life

_____

_____

_____

_____

_____

_____

_____

_____

MAY 30

If someone had told me ten years ago that I would be living my dream, writing and painting every day, happily married and fulfilled, I would have thought they were crazy, but here I am. Sometimes life gets very hard and somewhere along the line you hit rock bottom. All you can do is stand there and look up to where the light is, wishing there were some way out. I'm living proof that life gets better and there were many times when I thought it never, never would, but tiny successes turn into larger ones.

Anne Tiller Slates

You see things;
and you say "Why?"
But I dream things that
never were;
and I say "Why not?"

George Bernard Shaw

Footnotes for Life

_____

_____

_____

_____

_____

_____

_____

The world seems impatient with time. Children can't wait to grow up. Grownups wish time had not passed so quickly. Older ones wish for "the good old days." In all of this process, no one seems to enjoy the present stage of life. Instead of living one day at a time many live in guilt from yesterday or dread of tomorrow.

Today is the time to love, laugh, encourage, smile and to cheer the faint-hearted. It's the time to leave a good memory, to say, "I love you," and to forgive a wrong. This very day is the day to give appreciation to someone you have long admired. Today is the time of your life!

> *Be patient toward all that is unsolved in your heart and try to love the questions themselves.*
>
> Rainer Maria Rilke

Joan Clayton

Footnotes for Life

_____

_____

_____

_____

_____

_____

_____

_____

Wrestling with your mind weakens you. When negative thoughts grab hold of you, observe them without judgment and they will loosen their grip. To remain cheerful, learn how to cordon off areas of weakness. Once you refuse them entry into the rest of your mind, they can no longer influence you. Then you can work on them safely.

Brahma Kumaris
World Spiritual University

The secret of success lies in the balance of remaining firm in the goals you set, but flexible in the process of realizing them.

Brahma Kumaris

Footnotes for Life

_____

_____

_____

_____

_____

_____

_____

_____

JUNE 2

Laughter reveals a childlike trust that all will eventually be well. All may not seem well at the present moment. Things may not line up in as orderly a fashion as I would prefer, but believing that my Higher Power is at the helm, I can ease my heart with the healing nourishment of laughter as I set my hand to doing whatever can be done.

Rhonda Brunea

With the fearful strain that is on me day and night, if I did not laugh I should die.

Abraham Lincoln

Footnotes for Life

_____

_____

_____

_____

_____

_____

_____

O n this new morning shed your anxiety and fears; treat this day as a new adventure. Streamline your daily routine and leave more time for you. Pace your wants and needs and let yourself be less than perfect. The major roadblock in your life has been cleared and you need to establish those new boundaries. Remember to look within yourself and revitalize your thinking. Take a moment for quiet reflection. Once you're confident and motivated you'll empower your survivor qualities. They were always there, but now they need to be recharged. Congratulate yourself and breathe in your tranquil state of mind.

Most true happiness comes from one's inner life. It takes reflection and contemplation and self-discipline.

William L Shirer

Suzanne Baginskie

Footnotes for Life

_____

_____

_____

_____

_____

_____

_____

_____

JUNE 4

I choose not to let myself become a victim of circumstance. I refuse to let fear stop me from taking a chance. I understand time and persistence is the pathway to my goal and although I will encounter obstacles, I'll not let go of my dream.

I know that faith in God will give me strength from within and I accept that I may sometimes need help from others. If there is a day I fall short of the finish line I'll remind myself that I have tomorrow to make it in record time. I know that in every field, the expert was once a beginner and I recognize within myself and others the potential of being a winner!

Teri Mitchell

Have confidence that if you have done a little thing well, you can do a bigger thing well, too.

Joseph Storey

Footnotes for Life

_____

_____

_____

_____

_____

_____

_____

One cold icy night my life changed forever. I was sitting in the car with the motor running waiting for my son to finish a court-ordered A.A. meeting when a young woman knocked on my window. "Why don't you come in and share a cup of coffee with us?" I climbed out and we hurried inside. The topic was detachment. I didn't have a clue what that meant, but as I listened an overwhelming sense of belonging washed over me. I was not alone. I was not crazy. My son's grown now and sober but I still attend Al-Anon. It's not about him, it's about me and sometimes I get the two mixed up and I need the wisdom to know the difference.

Convincing yourself does not win the argument.

Robert Half

Carol Davis Gustke

Footnotes for Life

JUNE 6

The gift of friendship can be hard to accept. I wonder, "Is there a string attached? What is that person's motive?" I need to learn to be a gracious acceptor of what is offered to me. I can analyze the person, the friendship and the words. Accepting the friendship slowly and cautiously can help me begin to trust others. There are those who might attempt to take advantage of me, but I still need to take the time to examine the offer. Caution and time can be my friends.

Linda Myers-Sowell

It is more shameful to distrust our friends than to be deceived by them.

La Rochefoucauld

Footnotes for Life

_____

_____

_____

_____

_____

_____

_____

_____

JUNE 7

I have grown beyond the need to prove to anyone that I am a good girl. I am not waiting to be rescued or saved. I do not require anyone's permission to be who I am. I am learning not to experience myself as a child. The source of my approval resides within me and not at the mercy of others. I have the ability to see the normal frictions of everyday life in a realistic perspective and not translate them into evidence of rejection or of my not really being loved. Along with my autonomy, I am respecting other people's needs to follow their own destinies, to be alone sometimes, to be preoccupied with issues not involved with me. I have matured and embrace my independence.

There is no failure except in no longer trying.

Elbert Hubbard

Rokelle Lerner

Footnotes for Life

JUNE 8

Often the appearance of something is not really that thing at all, but rather the lack of something else. For what is darkness but the absence of light? Sorrow but the absence of joy? Hate but the absence of love? Lack but the absence of abundance? There is no lack in God. Embrace abundance.

Today I release old thoughts, patterns or habits that impede my life experience. I open, totally and completely, to a divine abundance of good in all areas of my life.

Jeffrey R. Anderson

If we share with caring and love, we will create abundance and joy for each other.

Deepak Chopra, M.D.

Footnotes for Life

_____

_____

_____

_____

_____

_____

_____

_____

Cars rust. Rusting must start inside some-where. Then it just pops out in spots through the paint. Once it starts, it goes fast, from a speck to many specks to a whole part. It's the same with addicts. Rusty cars are hard to remember new. Their vexations blot out the memory of their charm, their accessories and even particular model year. It takes concentration to call up the original image. It's the same with alcoholics. Old cars begin to look alike, inside and out, but they get the job done again and again. They gain respect, a place in the family, and even acceptance and understanding of frequent breakdowns. It's the same with addicts and alcoholics.

Courage is a quality so necessary for maintaining virtue that it is always respected.

Samuel Johnson

Joseph R. Cruse

Footnotes for Life

_____

_____

_____

_____

_____

_____

_____

_____

JUNE 10

Despite the miracle in my life, recovery remains a day-to-day process. It began with the supernatural power to forgive and it continues with a grateful and ever repentant heart.

Miracles do happen. Seekers do get healed. Lives can be forever changed. Recovery is not just a road, it is also a reason.

Rev. Ed Donnally

It is faith in something and enthusiasm for something that makes life worth looking at.

Oliver Wendell Holmes

Footnotes for Life

_____

_____

_____

_____

_____

_____

_____

Each day produces a fresh opportunity to make new choices. Sometimes my past throws a shadow over the present. A fresh outlook, a new attitude and the determination to cast off the old weights will brighten my path through recovery. I learn to dodge, scale and push through the barriers that block the road to success. Continually looking over my shoulder makes it difficult to avoid the stumbling blocks in my path or to recognize and embrace the new plans for my future. I look forward to tomorrow. The best part of life might be just on the horizon.

Valerie Frost

Goals give you more than a reason to get up in the morning; they are an incentive to keep you going all day.

Harvey Mackay

Footnotes for Life

_____

_____

_____

_____

_____

_____

_____

_____

Natural anger is meant to protect me from harm and help me to know how I feel. In the past, I learned to stuff my own anger and I lost track of my own responses to situations because I denied my feelings before I knew I had them. Today I let myself have my angry feelings without letting them have me. I needn't let the feeling flood me or make me feel I need to react. I let my anger inform me that something is not okay so that I can be honest with myself and with others.

He who has been angry becomes cool again.

Greek Proverb

Tian Dayton

Footnotes for Life

_____

_____

_____

_____

_____

_____

_____

I believe the day I stopped trying to get over the loss of my mother was the day I truly began to heal. Sometimes we can't recover the person we used to be. By accepting our new persona we acquire the ability to get on with our lives—to live with new hopes and new skills.

Elva Stoelers

God grant me the serenity to accept the things I cannot change; the courage to change the things I can; and the wisdom to know the difference.

Reinhold Niebuhr

Footnotes for Life

_____

_____

_____

_____

_____

_____

_____

_____

JUNE 14

Don't deny sorrow and pretend that it doesn't exist. Just know that with sorrow comes hope to nurture our inner strength. Hope is healing, hope is Overcoming our problems and pain. Hope rests in the Perseverance that we portray in the face of adversity and quite simply hope is Everywhere. We hope to recover and we recover through hope . . . for sometimes hope is all we have.

Elizabeth Batt

Things never go so well that one should have no fear, and never so ill that one should have no hope.

Turkish Proverb

Footnotes for Life

_____

_____

_____

_____

_____

_____

_____

Our little girl lost her valiant five-month battle with a brain stem tumor only weeks before her birthday, a day which dawned fittingly with a steadily falling rain. I secluded myself. The tears and questions flowed. The answers didn't. Suddenly the sun peeked out, brilliant rays streamed through the window. I noticed a dark-eyed junco's nest in the porch rafters and the bird flying in "protect mode." As the mother bird made its third descent, thinking to comfort it, I said aloud, "Don't worry Mama Bird, your babies are safe." Those words echoed in my heart as if God had spoken them. I cried. Only this time, the tears were tears of joy.

I believe that laughter is the only cure for grief, and that love is stronger than death.

Robert Fulghum

Loretta McCann Bjorvik

Footnotes for Life

_____

_____

_____

_____

_____

_____

_____

_____

JUNE 16

Throughout my childhood, I dreamt of a peaceful yellow room where I would sit and wait. For twenty years I thought that little yellow room was a dream, some abstract defense mechanism to protect my psyche from the horrors of childhood sexual abuse. Abuse that destroyed trust, even in God. My guarded relationship with God changed through my Twelve-Step work. I hid in that little yellow room and I now know God built it lovingly, for me. He is a carpenter after all. He took hammer and nails, some sheetrock and a bucket of yellow paint that looked and felt like cool sunshine on a summer morning and created a safe place for me to wait.

As long as a man stands in his own way everything seems to be in his way.

Ralph Waldo Emerson

Shannon

Footnotes for Life

JUNE 17

At ten I was a member of a street gang, rising to the rank of leader. A series of drug and gang-related crimes led me to prison where I confronted my addictions and took an honest look at the choices I had made in my life. Functionally illiterate I reentered society through a prison-based, long-term residential drug treatment program. I have been sober for twenty years and a few years ago I received an award for "Counselor of the Year" out of eight thousand counselors in my state. My work is rewarding and I feel as if I make a difference in the lives of people I touch. No one knows the potential that lies dormant in those who cross our paths.

A dewy spider web, spun in silence proclaims, "I'm here by design!"

Rachel Blevins

Benneth Lee as told to Mark Sanders

Footnotes for Life

JUNE 18

Do not allow your ego to manipulate you into believing that your material or physical life is what matters. Always allow your spirit to decide what is important in your life. To follow the ego's path is to be empty, although if you follow the path of the spirit you will be eternally fulfilled. Today, try to seek what your spirit desires rather than what your ego demands. This choice between the ego and the spirit is the gift of recovery.

Rick Singer

An egotist is a person who plays too big a part in his own life.

Dan Bennett

Footnotes for Life

_____

_____

_____

_____

_____

_____

_____

_____

S hedding the shame of the judgments of others is like losing weight—it doesn't all come off at once. You may put some back on before you get to where you want to be. Just like that tempting chocolate cake in the back of the fridge, some people are waiting to fill you with regret and shame all over again. When you are strong and resist accepting the judgments of others, you feel lighter, brighter, able to do so many things you weren't doing before you lost it. It takes some work not to absorb those judgments; some exercise. And sometimes you've just got to clean out the fridge.

Carla Edmisten

It's not that some people have willpower and some don't. It's that some people are ready to change and others are not.

James Gordon, M.D.

Footnotes for Life

_____

_____

_____

_____

_____

_____

_____

_____

JUNE 20

When things were going too well, it was time to self-destruct again. Finally close friends and my wife urged me to complete a checklist that I often used with clients during their assessment for treatment. I did it to prove everyone wrong, but even with my background as a professional I was unprepared for my memories of sexual molestation. As my past began to unravel, there were times I wanted to deny it, but everywhere I turned my memories were being confirmed for me. I am not alone as a male survivor, but if it were not for my faith in God and my wife's faith in me, I would have given up. My life has started to make sense.

Stuart Brantley

He that will not apply new remedies must expect new evils, for time is the greatest innovator.

Francis Bacon

Footnotes for Life

_____

_____

_____

_____

_____

_____

_____

W hile in the process of "coming to believe," I realized that I had the wrong perspective about money. My money, as all things, belongs to my Higher Power. I am merely the agent responsible enough to see that it reaches its proper destination.

Sala Dayo

> *If money is all that a man makes, then he will be poor—poor in happiness, poor in all that makes life worth living.*
>
> Herbert N. Casson

Footnotes for Life

_____

_____

_____

_____

_____

_____

_____

_____

JUNE 22

There is no need to prove the truth. Trying to do so shows only your own stubbornness. Truth will always reveal itself at the right moment and the right place. You need be concerned only with living true to your own self. Judge whether your thoughts, words or actions are beneficial to the scene in which you find yourself. Focusing on your own part is more useful than passing judgment on others.

Brahma Kumaris
World Spiritual University

By constantly remaining obedient to your sense of integrity, certain success obeys your every move.

Brahma Kumaris

Footnotes for Life

JUNE 23

Set your roots down deep and drink from refreshing streams as you dine on the sustenance provided by the One who gives you life. Nourish yourself with words, values and relationships that will uphold you during the storms of life. Make right choices to move forward, leaving behind the floods and droughts of the past. Enjoy the refreshing rain of forgiveness as it washes away the dirt from each day. Sway with gentle breezes, bend with fierce winds, and reach to the highest heights as you bask in the warmth of the sun.

Ava Pennington

Life is simplified when there is one center, one reason, one motivation, one direction and purpose.

Jean Fleming

Footnotes for Life

_____

_____

_____

_____

_____

_____

_____

_____

To "live in the moment" means to breathe the fragrance of Heaven, to stop and listen to the cry of need, to step out in faith and love bringing God's provision, to not miss it all because I'm too busy running to the next moment.

Karen Hall

We have stopped for a moment to encounter each other. To meet, to love, to share. It is a precious moment, but it is transient. It is a little parentheses in eternity.

Deepak Chopra, M.D.

Footnotes for Life

_____

_____

_____

_____

_____

_____

_____

_____

Loved ones of a suicide often blame themselves, but I don't. I know the choices my husband made in his life were his choices, not mine. Because of my faith in a loving, merciful God and because I have experienced many difficult trials in my life, I have learned how to survive and choose to survive well. I am fully alive and I believe my late husband is also. He was a man who loved his family and who is no longer burdened by a disease that had him in its awful grip. I take one day at a time, enjoy the rain and the sun, endure the ice and the freezing winds— and feel peace.

Ann Best

The only useless endeavor is to resist the command knit into our very souls, move. Move on.

Unknown

Footnotes for Life

_____

_____

_____

_____

_____

_____

_____

_____

JUNE 26

We play a variety of roles in life, but we should not depend on roles to define ourselves. A role always involves someone else's needs, expectations and agendas, which may have little to do with our own. The power of a role lies in its "possessive other": parents' child; children's parent; boss's assistant; spouse's mate. His. Hers. Theirs. We must sometimes put the word "my" into that place of possessive power. "I am my . . . what?" What role do I play for me? Having no answer for that makes us as dependent as the sound of that old, proverbial tree falling in the forest—if there's no one around to hear us, our very existence becomes questionable.

Maribeth Pittman

Footnotes for Life

To know what you prefer instead of what the world tells you you ought to prefer, is to keep your soul alive.

Robert Louis Stevenson

Many years ago, while in detox, helpless and hopeless, I came to know the real meaning of true love—one drunk looking after another drunk. It was there that I learned that if I took certain simple steps, my life would improve in ways that I could not then imagine. These promises have become my reality.

Sobriety subtly makes itself manifest in my spirit. It is as though I have been given the chance to relive part of my life again. Only in retrospect does each year become gentler than the year before and the change is as inconspicuous as the beating of my heart.

Peter Wright

Man improves himself as he follows his path; if he stands still, waiting to improve before he makes a decision, he'll never move.

Paulo Coelho

Footnotes for Life

_____

_____

_____

_____

_____

_____

_____

_____

JUNE 28

While riding to a weekend recovery convention, my children heard the word "crackpot" on the radio and began incessantly joking, "You crackpot!" I focused on feeling the presence of my Higher Power and being grateful for the kids. The breakup of a relationship bore heavily on me and one of my intentions that weekend was to process my emotional pain after the loss of my dream romance. In a serendipitous moment, the final workshop speaker told a Zen story of blooming that resulted from water dripping from an imperfect "cracked pot." The "God-incidence" of hearing those uncommon words again tickled my soul. I headed home with a mending heart, mindful of the joy recovery brings to my life.

Coincidence is when God chooses to remain anonymous.

Unknown

Pamela Knight

Footnotes for Life

As I gain an understanding about food and it no longer controls me, a sense of power arises. I replace eating for other non-injurious pleasures: new activities, new friendships, rediscovering creativity.

My ability to distinguish physical hunger from emotional hunger grows and this growth makes it less possible to fool myself that filling up my stomach fills up my heart.

Donna LeBlanc

Experience is a hard teacher because she gives the test first, the lesson afterward.

Vernon Law

Footnotes for Life

_____

_____

_____

_____

_____

_____

_____

_____

Behind the giggles, eight-year-old Amanda struggled with her mother's steady descent into the abyss of alcoholism. Although they were separated, Amanda's dad respected the deep bond she had for her mother. He encouraged Amanda to understand and cope with the family's circumstances. She quickly learned she was not alone, that millions of other kids love parents challenged by alcoholism and other drug addiction. She was relieved to know she didn't make her mother drink and more importantly, couldn't make her stop. With Dad's loving act and his extraordinary commitment he gave his little girl the gift he himself had been denied as a child—a safe place to grow, learn and heal.

If they drop the atom bomb, if I want to have a chance at survival, I want to be with a bunch of ACoAs.

Cathleen Brooks

Jerry Moe

Footnotes for Life

When we call something by its right name, we have stopped pretending. We are facing the truth, refusing to dress up what we see. It is then that life is put in perspective, and we begin to understand.

Only after we call things by their right names do we have the privilege of renaming them.

Barbara A. Croce

The beginning of wisdom is to call things by their right names.

Traditional Chinese Proverb

Footnotes for Life

_____

_____

_____

_____

_____

_____

_____

_____

JULY 2

May all your days be blessed with someone who cares for you, accepts you and your flaws, who will watch over you and protect you. Someone who will encourage you to believe in life and in your wishes and dreams, who will give you strength and guidance and care for you throughout eternity.

Stacey Chillemi

The curious paradox is that when I accept myself just as I am, then I can change.

Carl Rogers

Footnotes for Life

_____

_____

_____

_____

_____

_____

_____

As you do, so you become. Every action that you perform is recording in you, the soul. These imprints ultimately mold your character and destiny. When you understand this principle, you will pay more attention to bringing your best to everything you do. React less; respond more. As you learn to tell your mind what to do, old ways of thinking and doing will change.

Brahma Kumaris
World Spiritual University

Whenever life throws you a curve ball, remember this is all just a game.

Brahma Kumaris

Footnotes for Life

_____

_____

_____

_____

_____

_____

_____

_____

JULY 4

Whispers solve a lot of problems. You can't argue in a whisper. You have to listen carefully to hear a whisper. "Whispers" in the night make everything right. What seemed so gigantic in the brightness of the day loses its significance in the security of a whisper. How do I know? In fifty-seven years of marriage, my husband's whispers in the wee hours of the morning have brought a lifetime of "I love you's." Love lies behind a whisper. Love always triumphs. Love wins over all. The next misunderstanding can end with a whisper. Whisper today. It works every time.

Before you speak,
ask yourself, is it kind,
is it necessary, is it true,
does it improve on the
silence?

Sai Baba

Joan Clayton

Footnotes for Life

Ida was the cleaning lady. I was the new admission. As she worked, she asked why I was there. "I lost my wedding band and my sanity last week. I'm trying to calm down," I explained. "You should talk to St. Anthony. He finds things when you ask," she offered kindly. The next day she persisted, obviously serious about this saint thing. Unfamiliar with saints, prayer, even dumb luck, I wrote St. Anthony a poem. Days later while cleaning the garage my husband walked inside with shaking hands—and my ring. "It fell out of an empty six-pack container," he said. I don't know if St. Anthony was impressed with my poetry, but I knew Ida believed and had lent me both her belief and her favorite saint.

Carol J. Bonomo

We are each of us angels with only one wing, and we can only fly by embracing one another.

Luciano de Crescenzo

Footnotes for Life

JULY 6

Recovering from an illness or from some dreaded disease of the heart or mind—from alcoholism, drug addiction or abuse—can scar us but they cannot destroy our spirit, not if we refuse to allow it. It takes great courage to believe that we can overcome. There is a certain bravery in facing up to our own weaknesses, to our own mortality, to all of the possibilities that might be visited upon us. Life is what it's all about. Life is taking a stand with someone, loving through the hardships, encouraging the defeated, teaching the young. And in the simple touch of a hand or a warm embrace we heal each other, one person at a time.

Todd Outcalt

Find a purpose in life so big it will challenge every capacity to be at your best.

David O. McKay

Footnotes for Life

_____

_____

_____

_____

_____

_____

_____

Growing up, my husband's house was "party central." It was so bad his neighbors nicknamed his cul-de-sac "alcoholic's circle." The first time Rich brought me home to meet Mom, she was so drunk she was sliding out of the chair and spoke with slurred speech. I was shocked. Later he calmly explained, "Didn't I tell you? My mom's a party girl." He could have said she was a drunk or a loser, but he didn't. He accepted her for who she was. When people complain about their alcoholic I tell them what I learned from my husband, "Quit trying to change them and try some compassion. Life is a lot more peaceful that way."

Carla Riehl

As I surrendered my imaginary power over others, I gained a more realistic view of my own life.

Al-Anon World Service

Footnotes for Life

_____

_____

_____

_____

_____

_____

_____

_____

JULY 8

The more I learn the more I know that I do not understand. Life is full of new and wonderful information; paradoxes and confusion abound; every new idea leads to a further truth and the journey seems endless.

In a sense we are all disciples; we are all learning from each other and the role of teacher and student is forever being exchanged. In my sobriety I am able to see how many wonderful "things" exist in the world; so many fascinating and interesting places to visit, so many loving and insightful people. God has given me much. I am so grateful to be able to learn in His garden.

To teach is to learn.

Japanese Proverb

Reverend Leo Booth

Footnotes for Life

_____
_____
_____
_____
_____
_____
_____
_____

My graduation dress made a surprise appearance from the back of my closet last spring. I heard the faint rattle of bones as the skeleton I had zipped into the folds of yellow chiffon was suddenly released. I had never admitted to anyone that I was bulimic; not my teenage daughters, nor my mother, who died never knowing my secret. As I eyed the soft fabric in my lap I realized that eating disorders never disappear, they simply shuffle themselves to the backs of closets and lurk. Now that the skeleton is out of my closet, I hope I can learn to accept the teenager who wore that dress and forgive her the dark secret she's been hiding.

> *Truth has a healing effect, even when not fully understood.*
>
> Mary Baker Eddy

Elva Stoelers

Footnotes for Life

JULY 10

Through the years, I have channeled my anger in many ways . . . in order not to face it. I have used competence as a weapon, exercising my power by becoming a taskmaster. I have vented my anger by using chemicals or food, abusing myself and others by my erratic, destructive behavior. I was led to believe that if I cut myself off from my rage, it would go away. Today I know that it is precisely from cutting myself off from my emotions that I lack skills in resolving them. I am learning how to turn to others for assistance and support to resolve my emotions without letting my anger run my life.

Rokelle Lerner

The fly cannot be driven away by getting angry at it.

African Proverb

Footnotes for Life

It calls to me, like an angry father calling a child. I don't want to go, but feel powerless to resist. It is an addiction, my addiction. It's in my blood and clouds my judgment, but not my heart.

This is my struggle, my fight, and I will win. Alcoholism may wage a war, but it will not take me prisoner. We are not alone in this battle. Together we will find the strength to overcome an enemy that does not like to be ignored. Day by day, one step at a time.

Raquel Strand

Destiny is not a matter of chance; it is a matter of choice. It is not a thing to be waited for; it is a thing to be achieved.

William Jennings Bryan

Footnotes for Life

_____

_____

_____

_____

_____

_____

_____

_____

JULY 12

Finding myself in prison was both the worst and the best thing that ever happened to me. I was nothing but a number to the prison system, but Carla, my counselor in the court-ordered drug program, always treated me with respect and dignity. When I finally walked out of prison I was convinced I would put that part of my life completely out of my mind. It hasn't quite worked out that way. In my day-to-day living when I get a little shaky in my recovery I still hear Carla's warm voice telling me, "I am so proud of you, you've earned this," or feel her hug, as loving as if she were my own mother. You can find angels everywhere.

Christine Learmonth

A true friend never gets in your way—unless you happen to be going down.

Anonymous

Footnotes for Life

_____

_____

_____

_____

_____

_____

_____

_____

Forgiveness is not about weakness. It's about freedom and strength. The strong and courageous face the reality that forgiveness needs to happen for their own sakes more than for the sake of the ones who caused the pain. Forgiveness says, "I am not responsible to seek my own justice. I choose to let life's consequences and the Almighty God deal with you." Then the forgiver steps forward in life, having removed the chains that held her to the ones who caused the pain. Neither they, nor the past, can harm her any longer.

Stephanie Ziebarth

Be kind, for everyone you meet is fighting a great battle.

Philo of Alexandria

Footnotes for Life

_____

_____

_____

_____

_____

_____

_____

_____

When we let go of the energy it takes to hold on to anger, blame and resentment, we have the energy to get our own needs met.

Feeling all the feelings and forgiving someone else is a gift we give to ourselves.

It's called serenity.

Sharon Wegscheider-Cruse

The weak can never forgive. Forgiveness is the attribute of the strong.

Mahatma Gandhi

Footnotes for Life

_____

_____

_____

_____

_____

_____

_____

_____

The process of self-transformation is not a ten-yard dash, but a one-hundred-fifty mile run. Patience makes the journey possible. It keeps you cool and calm. So pace yourself. Self-confidence is to know your way around yourself so instinctively that you always have a strength to draw on. Somewhere inside, from the stillness, you can always find something to meet your need.

Brahma Kumaris
World Spiritual University

Not repeating your mistakes is a form of progress.

Brahma Kumaris

Footnotes for Life

_____

_____

_____

_____

_____

_____

_____

_____

JULY 16

Today I will learn something new. I will open my mind to new ways of looking at the same old thing. I will intervene in my habitual, hypnotic patterns of thought that keep me doing the same thing over and over again. I will recognize that if I am going to feel truly alive I need to bring my renewed self to each day. Though my body will grow old, my brain can stay young and flexible through new learning.

Tian Dayton

Anyone who stops learning is old, whether at twenty or eighty. Anyone who keeps learning stays young. The greatest thing in life is to keep your mind young.

Henry Ford

Footnotes for Life

Sometimes our bodies fail us. And if our spirits fail us too, the world is full of brave people from whom we can grab a handful of courage. When I was very ill, I received weekly intravenous treatments for almost two years. Somewhere in the middle, I lost my courage. One day the search for a healthy vein became too painful. I pushed the needle away and cried. A young girl of about ten, who had battled cancer all her life, smiled at me and, lifting her T-shirt, showed me the hole that had been cut into her abdomen so that she could receive her treatments through a permanent plastic port. Then she put her hand, so small and soft, on mine and said, "You can take it." And I did.

There is strength in knowing that it can be borne, although it tears.

Emily Dickinson

Nancy Burke

Footnotes for Life

During a traumatic period in my life, I learned to elevate my spirits daily by concentrating on finding some reason to feel grateful. Many times I would start with someone else's life. I was always grateful that my children were healthy. I began to write down the blessings. The list grew, and as it grew, my health seemed to improve and my enthusiasm for life began to return.

Life is just a blank slate, what matters most is what you write on it.

Christine Frankland

I became aware of the genius of a Creator who designed our bodies, the intricacies of a respiratory system, our amazing hearts.

Now, I am happy to say that I am amazed at just how many miracles it takes to make an average day.

Nancy Eckerson

Footnotes for Life

_____

_____

_____

_____

_____

_____

There were times I thought that I would never survive the tension, the stress, the unresolved problems and unsatisfying relationships. But I look back and know that I have survived. I see that I remove myself from tense situations by letting go of the responsibility I feel to change other people and events. Ironically, serenity surrounds me if I don't avoid the barriers of over-responsibility that are thrown in my path. These barriers are my challenge, now and forever, and I accept that as a lesson in life. In challenging myself to conquer them, I reach new heights, new realms of self-determination and inner strength.

Rokelle Lerner

I will acknowledge rewards for they are my due; yet I will welcome obstacles for they are my challenge.

Og Mandino

Footnotes for Life

_____

_____

_____

_____

_____

_____

_____

_____

The flowers had an odd, unnatural appearance as the shopkeeper lifted them from their shipping box. Tiny nets captured the largest blooms, squeezing them inward like miniature straightjackets. She prepared a place for them and then patiently, gently, she pulled the netting away. With their bindings removed, the petals burst open, revealing hidden beauty and fragrance. Recovery removes the confinements that hinder me from experiencing life's full bloom.

Rhonda Brunea

> *A single rose can be my garden ... a single friend, my world.*
>
> Leo Buscaglia

Footnotes for Life

_____

_____

_____

_____

_____

_____

_____

I watched the rain bouncing on the sun deck through my kitchen window. I focused on heavy clouds and raindrops snaking down the glass as I absently washed the dishes. I settled on the dullness of the day and let my mood reflect the vision.

My melancholy was interrupted by the movement of a squirrel teetering on a brittle branch of our apple tree. An apple dangled like a Christmas ornament just beyond his grasp. I watched him lose his balance as he reached for it. Undaunted, he regained his footing and tried again. The branch swayed with his effort and the apple bounced to the ground, the squirrel in hot pursuit. As if by magic the view from my window began to drip with promise.

No rain–no rainbows.

Unknown

Elva Stoelers

Footnotes for Life

_____

_____

_____

_____

_____

_____

_____

_____

Fear holds my memories hostage. If I remember, I may break into a thousand pieces. Then I realize that I am already broken. Who was the person who disappeared when the abuse began?

I pick up a piece of memory here and another one there. I arrange the memories in correct order.

As I remember, I reassemble the sculpture of my life to its original design.

Darlene Franklin

The past is malleable and flexible, changing as our recollection interprets and re-explains what has happened.

Peter Berger

Footnotes for Life

_____

_____

_____

_____

_____

_____

_____

It is up to each of us to determine how we are going to recover from adversity or tragedy in our lives. It is easy to fall victim to the loss, to use it as an excuse for personal failure, emotional or social problems. My mother's death when I was eighteen was a tremendous obstacle for me to face, but I made a decision not to allow myself to be victimized by the loss. Being angry or questioning God left me feeling emptier than ever. Instead, having unwavering faith in him and trust in his greater purpose allowed me to find mine. I honor my mother's memory by being the person she raised me to be—the person she invested her life in.

However long the night, the dawn will break.

African Proverb

Letitia Trimmer Meeks

Footnotes for Life

JULY 24

One moment. Now. The past is but a fragile web of regret and memory. The future is full of joys and sorrows that are yet to have substance. All that you can really touch is this moment. Savor this moment completely. Smell the wet grass. Listen to a loved one's laughter. Take the time to sip your coffee. Study the sunset from an overstuffed chair. Embrace what is good. Cherish what is pure. We cannot hoard yesterday. Neither can we spend tomorrow. We can only treasure today.

Renee Hixson

Do not dwell in the past, do not dream of the future, concentrate the mind on the present moment.

Buddha

Footnotes for Life

"Ours is a disease of attitudes." I recognize that my negative attitudes hamper my recovery path. The negative thinking and destructive attitudes that I learned growing up with addiction and dysfunction remain with me until I do something to change them. Forcing positivity on top of negativity does not work, neither side rings true when I do that. What I need to do is remember that I have trouble with my attitudes and that I need special work in that area to restore them to sanity. Acknowledging the problem, sharing it out loud and turning it over helps. As I rework my past issues, I will remember that I need to make constant attitude adjustments so that I can maintain the good work that I am doing.

Be led by reason.

Greek Proverb

Tian Dayton

Footnotes for Life

JULY 26

Why do we destroy our emotional well-being with members of the opposite sex who will never be relationship material? Sound familiar? Then chances are you've heard the word "codependent" before. Seems as if we put more thought into our next meal than in choosing our mate. I, for one, would like to start with an appetizer of romance and thoughtfulness, with a dash of passion. For the main course, I'll have an emotionally stable, commitment-oriented, dependable, trustworthy, considerate, all-around decent guy, please! Oh, and can I have a side order of good communication skills to go with that?

Linda S. Day

Flatter me, I may not believe you. Criticize me, I may not like you. Ignore me, I may not forgive you. Encourage me, I will not forget you.

William Arthur Ward

Footnotes for Life

_____

_____

_____

_____

_____

_____

_____

There is a part of you that is perfect and pure. It is untouched by the less-than-perfect characteristics you have acquired by living in a less-than-perfect world. This part of you is a still and eternal pool. Making time to reach it will bring you untold benefit. Your physical identity is a world of limited thoughts, feelings and roles. It is quite apart from the being of inner peace and power that is your spiritual personality.

Brahma Kumaris
World Spiritual University

You have the key to unlock a direct connection with God—and that key is self-respect.

Brahma Kumaris

Footnotes for Life

_____

_____

_____

_____

_____

_____

_____

_____

JULY 28

My lungs ached as I climbed what seemed to be a vertical path until three hours later I reached the top. To the east lay the broad expanse of a valley—its emerald lake cradled by the rugged Rockies. But to the west, was one more summit. It seemed impossible to go any farther, but with grueling determination, I climbed on. At the crest I beheld a vista of three glorious valleys, their splendor breathtaking; an image that is forever etched in my memory. In life, never quit when there's one more summit, the reward at the top is worth every ounce of pain along the way.

Linda Mehus-Barber

In order to succeed we must first believe that we can.

Michael Korda

Footnotes for Life

_____

_____

_____

_____

_____

_____

_____

JULY 29

Attitude is everything or so it seems. It determines the outcome of what life brings. So never look beyond yourself for answers to your prayers.

Instead, look inside your heart, and you will find what you need right there.

Theresa Meehan

Nothing can stop the man with the right mental attitude from achieving his goal; nothing on Earth can help the man with the wrong mental attitude.

W. W. Ziege

Footnotes for Life

_____

_____

_____

_____

_____

_____

_____

_____

As a child in an alcoholic home, I made decisions impulsively and the results were inconsistency, chaos and unpredictability. I must make choices in my recovery and I must act on them, but I must think before I act. This is not indecisiveness, but rather a disciplined decision to avoid impulsiveness in my behavior. When I try to satisfy my desires without success, I take the time to listen to my inner voice. When I am concerned by what people think, say or do, I pause and decide what I really want. I think before I act and take my thoughts seriously.

Thought is the blossom; language the bud; action the fruit behind it.

Ralph Waldo Emerson

Rokelle Lerner

Footnotes for Life

Every few years, I drag out the pine box with brass hinges I made in seventh-grade wood shop. There between my second-grade report card and a poem from a high school girlfriend, are the two photos of Calvin and Allen, friends from long ago. They had so much in common, loving families, doing well in school and in athletics. Another similarity had the greatest impact—both became entangled in the terror of drug addiction. Allen overdosed at twelve and Calvin never saw his twentieth birthday. So, periodically I bring out the box, dust off the photos and hope I've learned what I need to prevent history from repeating itself with my two children who mean everything to me.

Good people come to wisdom through failure.

William Saroyan

David R. Wilkins

Footnotes for Life

_____

_____

_____

_____

_____

_____

_____

Be grateful for what you have at this moment in your life and you will feel a sense of calm. Sit in a quiet place. Write the words, "Today, I am grateful for . . .", then write what comes to mind. You may be grateful that you have these few moments to sit quietly. You may be grateful for the kind words of a friend or for the life of someone close to you. There are many tangible things to be grateful for that can be easily over-looked: a warm bath, a cool drink, a comfortable chair to sink into. When we practice gratitude, we begin to accept our lives and ourselves. Be good to yourself, practice gratitude.

We need to be grateful for many things that did not happen.

Langenhoven

Barbara Elizabeth Lowell

Footnotes for Life

_____

_____

_____

_____

_____

_____

_____

_____

AUGUST 2

Standing in line at our town post office impatiently waiting for my turn, I noticed a woman struggling to get through the door because she was carrying so many packages. She stood next to me. I noticed that no one volunteered to help her and I was thinking, "I can't believe these people just don't want to lose their precious place in line." A voice inside me told me that I could help—but that I too would lose my place in line. Believing, however, that I am a person who does help, I volunteered to hold some of her packages. Did I learn anything that day? Yes, sometimes to do the right thing you need to get out of line.

Robert J. Ackerman

If you think about what you ought to do for other people, your character will take care of itself.

Woodrow Wilson

Footnotes for Life

_____

_____

_____

_____

_____

_____

_____

I believe that life wants to work out if we let it. I believe that God is in charge and that if we hold that thought and release it every time it occurs to us, good things will follow. I believe life is a gift and that it is my responsibility to work it till it works. I believe that a good attitude is worth more than money, a good heart is worth more than a high birth and that a good character is a foundation upon which at least three generations can be built. I believe in love and its power to heal, restore and reveal our next lessons. I believe in the gift of recovery in my life.

Tian Dayton

Shared joy is joy doubled. Shared sorrow is sorrow halved.

Anonymous

Footnotes for Life

_____

_____

_____

_____

_____

_____

_____

_____

AUGUST 4

Some days you arise with a zestful feeling knowing a fresh new day is before you. Other days your first thought is of a problem, a fear or perhaps simply a mundane task awaiting you. Perhaps it's a rainy day outside, or perhaps it is a rainy day in your heart. Whether you are new or old to recovery dark days will come. Just as a squirrel stores up nuts, we should fill our pantry with nuggets of hope. A favorite poem or spiritual passage can lighten your mood. Uplifting music or physical activities can get our spirits and bodies moving in a positive direction.

Joyce McDonald Hoskins

Life is just a blank slate, what matters most is what you write on it.

Christine Frankland

Footnotes for Life

_____

_____

_____

_____

_____

_____

_____

_____

L ove is the most healing and therapeutic gift I can give myself. I don't have to reach outside of myself to find love—it already exists within me. My parents, my friends, my lovers may not have given me the love I need, but love has never left me. It is when I don't nurture myself that I frantically search for someone to love me. This desperation leaves me as I go inside myself, when I open the door of my heart and embrace myself in unconditional love.

Rokelle Lerner

The main source of good discipline is growing up in a loving family, being loved and learning to love in return.

Dr. Benjamin Spock

Footnotes for Life

_____

_____

_____

_____

_____

_____

_____

_____

AUGUST 6

God, let me see the ways you are working in my life today. Help me be ever mindful of your presence, and grateful for all the things you send me. Let me be open to the lessons that come my way, and let me treat every person the way you would treat me.

Use my voice to speak, use my hands to do your work. Help me to see every situation through your eyes.

Kelly L. Stone

Lord, make me an instrument of thy peace.

St. Francis of Assisi

Footnotes for Life

_____

_____

_____

_____

_____

_____

_____

Once you accept that you have "no control" over others, you begin to relax and take one moment at a time. This week whenever you start to feel tension in the pit of your stomach, say to your mind, "I have no control over what they choose. They have a right to choose whatever they think they need."

Experience the freedom from accepting what you already knew—you have no control over anyone but yourself. Have a busy week of getting on with your life rather than trying to get on with someone else's!

Lana Fletcher

How simple it is to see that all the worry in the world cannot control the future. How simple it is to see that we can only be happy now. And that there will never be a time when it is not now.

Gerald Jampolsky

Footnotes for Life

August 8

I realize that taking care of myself means different things in different situations—there is no one way to do it and that is why, as a concept, it is so hard to get a hold of. To think that if I do recovery perfectly, do it all just right, I will produce stress-free relationships is magical thinking. It is a repetition of my childhood fantasy that if I just tried a little harder or understood a little better, I could make my family well. When we talk about recovery, we are talking about life and life offers no guarantees. We do what we can do and let go of the results. My real challenge in life is in expanding the interior of my own soul.

The nurse of full grown souls is solitude.

James Russell Lowell

Tian Dayton

Footnotes for Life

_____

_____

_____

_____

_____

_____

_____

_____

I have come to recognize that the person my resentments and grievances hurt most is me. So, if I wish to preserve my health and to enable my continuing recovery and growth, I must regularly practice forgiveness. When I do, I release those emotion-filled perceptions that otherwise will inhibit my ability to experience and express love and also will continue to color and poison my relationships and interactions with others. The benefits are enormous—immediately, a "lightness" of spirit, and over time, greater serenity and joy.

Always forgive your enemies, nothing annoys them so much.

Oscar Wilde

Jeff McFarland

Footnotes for Life

_____

_____

_____

_____

_____

_____

_____

_____

AUGUST 10

Discouraged and disheartened, I stood on the dusty roadside, my journey nearly half over, my reserves of strength and will ebbing away in the searing summer heat. Should I turn back now, or continue to an uncertain fate? As I deliberated, a tiny ant labored in the dry powdery dust. Just like me, he was scuffling and stumbling along, yet he pressed forward with dogged determination toward an unknown goal. I watched with silent fascination until he finally reached the edge of the road. What great fortitude! Inspired, I mustered the courage and determination to move ahead and complete my own journey. That tiny ant's example set me on a sure course out of poverty, homelessness and despair.

Life shrinks or expands in proportion to one's courage.

Anaïs Nin

David Claerr

Footnotes for Life

_____

_____

_____

_____

_____

_____

_____

Violence, sexual abuse, alcohol and drugs were the hallmarks of my life by the time I was fourteen. My path of self-destruction was my destiny. I married young and soon had two beautiful children, and that was the turning point in my life. I discovered that being a good mother was something I could accomplish. I faced my problems and learned healthy parenting and life skills. I faced the loathing and shame, and grieved for the loss of my childhood so that the cycle stopped with me. In its place a life centered on love and nurturing has taken root. I am careful to plant more seeds and water them daily.

Marilyn Joan

> *The most common sort of lie is the one uttered to one's self.*
>
> Friedrich Nietzsche

Footnotes for Life

_____

_____

_____

_____

_____

_____

_____

_____

AUGUST 12

Much of the incredible confusion of growing up with dysfunctional parents came from never knowing what they wanted. Our sense of self was nonexistent. We were important enough to be there when they felt good, but weren't important enough to be there when they didn't. We never learned to think of ourselves as successful, because we never knew when we would be praised and when we would be pushed away. As adults, we can give ourselves consistent acceptance and affirmation. We can learn to pay attention to what we want.

Come here. I love you. Go away. I can't stand you. We have visitors, so stay in your room.

James C.

Yvonne Kaye

Footnotes for Life

_____

_____

_____

_____

_____

_____

_____

_____

In the far recesses of my soul there is a place of quietness, of meeting of heart and mind; a place of deep serenity, of where my true love dwells; a place where I can breathe easy and be my own true self. It is there that I find freedom to speak the truth in love; there, where honesty abounds in all simplicity and humility and God is more than enough. No guile, no deceit, no pretense. Masks unveiled, and true self revealed. I have lost my way to this blessed place, O Lord. How I long for this sanctuary within. Will you take me there again?

Lilian Chee Sau Leng

God asks no man whether he will accept life. That is not the choice. You must take it. The only choice is how.

Henry Ward Beecher

Footnotes for Life

_____

_____

_____

_____

_____

_____

_____

_____

August 14

I have the strength to lift up the rugs of my life and see what emotions have been swept underneath. I acquire this strength by exploring the notion that my old ways of seeing things aren't the only ways to see and in doing so I discover and practice healthier ways of observing myself and others.

Donna LeBlanc

*Watch what you are
doing instead of
thinking about
what you are doing.
Seeing, not thinking,
is believing.*

Donna LeBlanc

Footnotes for Life

_____

_____

_____

_____

_____

_____

_____

Thoughts have a creative power of their own. I can see my thoughts come to life and I create the possibility of what I would like by first experiencing it in my mind. I visualize what I would like to have in my life in my mind's eye and accept what I see in my inner eye as being there for me. I am specific about what I see, smell, taste and feel, and accept it as fully as possible. I enjoy my vision, then let it go and move on in my day, releasing it with no thought of controlling it further. I let it happen if it is right for me in God's time and knowing all good things are possible for me.

Tian Dayton

If one advances confidently in the direction of his dreams, he will meet with a success unexpected in common hours.

Henry David Thoreau

Footnotes for Life

_____

_____

_____

_____

_____

_____

_____

_____

AUGUST 16

The reality may dawn on us only after exhausting years wasted in attempts to orchestrate the behavior of others. The truth is, it doesn't work. We may have the best motives and the most sensible suggestions but in the end, people will do as they please regardless of our good advice. What a tremendous relief it is to finally grasp this and drop the crushing load of minding others' business. We are then free to tend our own affairs and make this one life as pleasant as it can be.

Rhonda Brunea

Be not angry that you cannot make others as you wish them to be, since you cannot make yourself as you wish to be.

Thomas à. Kempis

Footnotes for Life

_____

_____

_____

_____

_____

_____

_____

AUGUST 17

I can do a great deal to impact my world for the better without making major lifestyle changes. I recognize that this world will change only when the people in it change. It is people who have the power to destroy or save this planet. Today I resolve to channel my personal power toward good, to open myself to be worked through and with. The world in which I live is my world; it is all that I have.

If I see myself as powerless, it will only depotentiate me and make me feel impotent. That is a position I choose not to take today.

Tian Dayton

There is only one thing that is fully our own and that is our will or purpose.

Epictetus, 1st century A.D.

Footnotes for Life

_____

_____

_____

_____

_____

_____

_____

_____

Y ou hear the familiar voice and footsteps coming down the hall. The door opens and his voice breaks off, questions in his eyes as he scans the room. Confusion and fear, the very look you dreaded, erode his half smile and you struggle to look loving, yet firm. The intervention has begun. You wonder if he'll ever again say, "I love you." Several days later when you drop by the treatment center to pick up his dirty laundry, there is a note attached. Tentatively you open it, "Thank you. I love you. I'm Ted—and I'm an alcoholic."

Jann Mitchell

I believe that man will not merely endure; he will prevail.

William Faulkner

Footnotes for Life

Take time to discover the eccentricities of your personality. As you come to an understanding of yourself, rejoice in the knowledge that God created you on purpose, for a purpose. Be willing to share yourself with others so that they might open up and begin their own healing process. Spend time with them, speaking encouraging words while listening to their hurt and pain. Share dreams, emotions, disappointments and victories. There's nothing more powerful in your own healing than comforting others and giving them the precious gift of your time.

Linda Mehus-Barber

The art of being yourself at your best is the art of unfolding your personality into the person you want to be.

Wilfred Peterson

Footnotes for Life

_____

_____

_____

_____

_____

_____

_____

_____

August 20

The jangling of keys and slamming of gates brought me back to the reality of the cold, crowded cell. A prison guard bellowed, "Get out here, crack head!" I rose, along with forty other women, none of us certain to whom the guard was talking. It was not me. It would be two years before I saw my children again and once I was released from prison I entered a residential treatment program. I was no longer afraid to die, I was afraid of living my life the way I was. God works in mysterious ways. Recovering addicts know that better than just about anyone else.

Mary Barr

A friend is one who walks in when others walk out.

Walter Winchell

Footnotes for Life

When I look out my window, I see the beauty of the world that God has created and the opportunities it holds.

His beauty includes me. I need to feel good about myself; I need to have hope. I must love myself and accept who I am.

I must succeed in order to be an inspiration to others, as others were for me.

Stacey Chillemi

> *Man is, and forever has been, God's reflection.*
>
> Mary Baker Eddy

Footnotes for Life

_____

_____

_____

_____

_____

_____

_____

_____

AUGUST 22

When we come into this world, the first thing we do is breathe in. Divine inspiration. When we leave this world, the last thing we do is breathe out. Everything in between is just gravy. It's all been taken care of. We leave home and we go home. Children of God. And if we really believe he holds us in the palm of his hand for the journey, then anything can be endured.

Nancy Burke

Sitting quietly, doing nothing, spring comes and the grass grows by itself.

Zenrin

Footnotes for Life

_____

_____

_____

_____

_____

_____

_____

When life caves in on me and I feel like giving up, I force myself to list twenty things I am thankful for. Sometimes it can be as lame as "fingers," or "a chair to sit on," but I keep going until I reach my magic number. Somehow by then I find myself in a different frame of mind. When I am thankful, I move from being pitiful to being powerful.

Barbara A. Croce

An attitude of gratitude creates blessings.

Sir John Templeton

Footnotes for Life

_____

_____

_____

_____

_____

_____

_____

_____

Drinking helped me deal with my depression. I drank myself into a stupor to numb my internal pain. Repeated efforts at treatment failed until my last admission when they rolled me into the trauma unit on a gurney and began by addressing my depression. Thirty-two days later, I came away with a clear understanding that the only way I was going to be successful in my recovery was to be more involved in my recovering community. I had occasion to visit that facility again, not as a patient, but as a guest. I was there to discuss a collaboration between their program and the new treatment center I had just opened. I remember once wondering if life was worth living. Now I know.

I welcome happiness as it enlarges my heart; I endure sadness for it opens my soul.

Og Mandino

Perry D. Litchfield

Footnotes for Life

_____

_____

_____

_____

_____

_____

_____

_____

"There are great, exciting adventures waiting for you out there!" This is what one of my good friends in recovery said to me after I told her I just got divorced. I wasn't feeling very enthusiastic about my life at that point. As time passed though, I was grateful for her perspective and her positive approach to something about which I didn't feel very optimistic. How grateful I am for the people, a philosophy and a way of life that helps me see the positive in any given situation.

Anne Conner

*The way I see it,
if you want the
rainbow, you gotta
put up with the rain.*

Dolly Parton

Footnotes for Life

_____

_____

_____

_____

_____

_____

_____

_____

AUGUST 26

Our life is today. When we lay our head on the pillow tonight, this day will never come back—this is a one-time deal.

We will miss it if we wait for the illusive perfection of tomorrow, next week or next year.

In the eternal scheme of things, today is just a shallow breath. But without each breath linked to another, we cannot fulfill our destiny.

Barbara A. Croce

All of us tend to put off living, dreaming of some magical rose garden over the horizon instead of enjoying the roses that are blooming outside our windows today.

Dale Carnegie

Footnotes for Life

_____

_____

_____

_____

_____

_____

_____

Standing at the bottom of the stairs, unable to put my foot on the first step, I had never been more tired or more depressed in my entire life. I had to use the bathroom and I couldn't get off the floor. Suddenly I saw myself, a young woman, hand on the rail, tears in my eyes, looking up. As I closed my eyes to banish the image, one foot made it to the first step. Two hands grabbed the rail and pulled me to the next step. With my eyes still closed I made it to the top of the stairs. Success. Incredible. The road to recovery really did begin with that first step.

Anne Tiller Slates

Do not wait for ideal circumstances, nor the best opportunities; they will never come.

Janet E. Stuart

Footnotes for Life

_____

_____

_____

_____

_____

_____

_____

_____

AUGUST 28

For nearly thirty years I had little contact with my family until, one day, the phone rang. My dad was dying. I harbored no illusions of making up for a lifetime lost, but hoped to make the most of what little time we had left. One afternoon after talking around the edges, I told him that I was sorry for all the time we had missed. He smiled, reached for my hands, closed his eyes and spoke softly. Listening to him, I laid my head in his lap and cried for the little girl he had left so many years ago. That day, he became my father again, and I, his daughter. The sunlight faded as we held each other, perhaps not for a lifetime, but at the very least, for a childhood.

The longer you carry a grudge the heavier it gets.

Unknown

Theresa Peluso

Footnotes for Life

When my sister, who suffered from both addiction and mental illness was murdered, I turned to my Higher Power and asked that simple question: *Why?* I felt the enormity of the vacuum of silence. I no longer felt any connection to the resilient part of who I thought I was. I wanted to be with those who knew the misery I was experiencing, so I accepted a position helping abused, hurt children. What I discovered was hope. Despite everything that life had dished out to them, these kids refused to throw in their cards. They kept striving. They kept dreaming. They kept living. I needed to remember to do that and I have. Together we have healed.

> *The way to happiness is to lose yourself in a cause greater than yourself.*
>
> Unknown

Patricia O'Gorman

Footnotes for Life

_____

_____

_____

_____

_____

_____

_____

_____

AUGUST 30

I was the model teenager trying desperately to gain my stepfather's approval and love, but I never seemed to succeed. With high school nearing an end, I recognized that nothing I could do would change his behavior. For his birthday, I found a meaningful card that represented all the hopes of my heart. I wasn't sure what would happen, but I took the risk of being vulnerable. A few days later I found a caring note from him, the first correspondence I could recall written in his hand to me. The more time I spent on seeking growth in forgiveness and in my own character, rather than trying to fix or improve others, the more things turned around for us.

Do not look back in anger, or forward in fear, but around in awareness.

James Thurber

Erin Hagman

Footnotes for Life

AUGUST 31

I cut—any part of my body covered by clothes, although my wrists were my body part of choice. The slashes became my words, the only way I knew to express myself, a way of denying my sexual abuse. I cut not to feel. Cutting left me in a dull trance, entirely calm, numb and empty. Even in a society where so much has lost its shock value, cutting remains scandalous. It's been three years since I last cut. Because of those who helped me peel away my layers of defenses to understand what was at the root of my fears and pain, because of them, I am finally alive.

Elizabeth Walton

The rung of a ladder was never meant to rest upon, but only hold a man's foot long enough to enable him to put the other somewhat higher.

Thomas Henry Huxley

Footnotes for Life

_____

_____

_____

_____

_____

_____

_____

_____

Many small steps make a journey. When stuck in a dispirited state of mind, take one step to move yourself forward. Get out of bed. Walk your dog. Smile at a stranger.

No matter how insignificant that step may seem, your action will create a course of hope on which to proceed. As momentum soars, so will your spirit.

Vicki Graf

> *When there is no wind, row.*
>
> Chinese Proverb

Footnotes for Life

_____

_____

_____

_____

_____

_____

_____

_____

A woman lives with an abusive husband. She hates her life. She is angry and unhappy. She remains with the abuser another day.

A teenager is grossly overweight and is teased by classmates. He hates his life. He is angry and unhappy. He overeats another day.

A man drinks, gets into fights and ends up in jail often. He hates his life. He is angry and unhappy. He drinks another day.

Today we must learn from our mistakes of the past and go down a different path or we will surely end up in the same place as yesterday.

Kay Conner Pliszka

Insanity is doing the same thing over and over again and expecting different results.

Albert Einstein

Footnotes for Life

Wе enjoy living at the edge of town. One night while sitting in the living room we heard sounds on our front porch. My husband turned on the porch light and there stood seven little sheep all in a row, staring as if to say, "Will you please help us?" Emmitt opened the gate to the backyard and safely enclosed those cute little balls of wool until he could find the owner. Emmitt, unknowingly, became their shepherd for a while. The sheep followed him around wherever he went, displaying their trust and dependence. Without a shepherd, sheep are in danger. Without the Good Shepherd, so am I.

Joan Clayton

It is only destined by your attitude where you will end up in life. Don't let yourself get lost in the crowd.

Angela Duvall

Footnotes for Life

_____

_____

_____

_____

_____

_____

_____

_____

SEPTEMBER 4

I don't want to minimize the seriousness of money dysfunction, but I use humor as a tool to help me recover from it. Humor is a valuable part of our rediscovery. To be so deadly serious about getting well is a real bummer. We can have fun looking back at the things we did trying to balance our accounts. How many of us put money into a savings account and get so excited that we're earning 5% interest, completely overlooking the fact that we owe $10,000 on credit cards at 19.2%? I did all that. Now, I have to laugh. I am serious about my recovery, but I don't take it or myself too seriously.

Money doesn't always bring happiness. People with $10 million are no happier than people with $9 million.

Hobart Brown

Yvonne Kaye

Footnotes for Life

_____

_____

_____

_____

_____

_____

_____

It's important that when I experience problems, I remember that solutions are close at hand. Knowing this starts the flow of ideas needed to solve my problems. Changes do not just "happen." Solutions involve drastic changes in thought and expectations. Solutions require action and when I have a positive attitude, I can tackle any issue. Today I know I am free. I can use my freedom to indulge in all kinds of negative beliefs, or I can use my freedom to discipline my mind and concentrate on finding answers to my difficulties. The decision is mine to choose my experiences.

Rokelle Lerner

> *Do not now seek the answers, which cannot be given to you because you will not be able to live them. And the point is, to live everything. Live the questions now.*
>
> Rainer Maria Rilke

Footnotes for Life

_____

_____

_____

_____

_____

_____

_____

_____

SEPTEMBER 6

Illness is a chance to teach the mind to remain independent of physical circumstances and thus to connect with our inner resources.

Experiencing these qualities is a powerful medicine.

Hope, enthusiasm and wisdom are to the mind as food is to the body.

Everyone needs daily sustenance.

Brahma Kumaris
World Spiritual University

The trick to problem solving is to get to the root of the problem before the rest of it shows up.

Brahma Kumaris

Footnotes for Life

_____

_____

_____

_____

_____

_____

_____

_____

To feel fear is human, but we must never allow fear to halt our forward momentum in the healing way. Sometimes the thing we must do is frightening. It's challenging, difficult, different from anything we've known before. But rather than give up and slide backward, we do well to gather our little shreds of courage and forge ahead—fear or no fear—remembering the presence, goodwill and help of our Higher Power. We must do the thing, though we do it trembling. I will not let the emotion of fear hinder my growth. I will trust that I am being led and keep moving forward.

When I am afraid, I will trust in you.

Psalm 56:3, NIV

Rhonda Brunea

Footnotes for Life

_____

_____

_____

_____

_____

_____

_____

_____

SEPTEMBER 8

Today is a plowing day. I will dig deep within the soil of my heart and prepare the dirt for what is to come.

Even good seed cannot fulfill its purpose in hard, uncultivated ground, but when sown in dirt that has been worked, it will flourish and explode with fruit.

Don't ask me about the harvest quite yet; I am still pushing the plow.

Barbara A. Croce

The real issue is not whether to grow, it is how to grow and for what purpose.

Unknown

Footnotes for Life

_____

_____

_____

_____

_____

_____

_____

Stop looking at things as endings, look at them as beginnings. Change is scary; the unknown is frightening but only because we can't see what's coming next. Take a step forward, one at a time, to build your courage. Soon you won't hesitate. That one step may be full of fears but still you move forward. Open yourself to experiencing whatever it is life has for you at any given moment; a beautiful spring morning, the wonders of a gentle snowfall, the joyful sound of children playing in a schoolyard, the simple pleasure of just being able to draw another breath.

The greatest thing you'll ever learn is just to love and be loved in return.

Eden Ahbez

Aingeal Stone

Footnotes for Life

_____

_____

_____

_____

_____

_____

_____

_____

Admitting that I was an alcoholic was a difficult first step, but it was only a first step. The admission wasn't enough. It felt flat. What was missing turned out to be acceptance.

Acceptance meant I had to move forward, tell others, ask for help, work on my sobriety.

Until I fully accepted and embraced this, I was emotionally paralyzed. Fear and shame held me captive. Acceptance has liberated me.

Deb Sellars Karpek

Life is what happens, after you make other plans.

Ralph Marston

Footnotes for Life

_____

_____

_____

_____

_____

_____

_____

_____

Following a loss, how do you grow a new heart? You don't. You work with the heart you have left. The missing parts can never be replaced. The bruised areas of the heart, however, have the ability to mend. It's not an easy or quick process. The balm is patience, support, acceptance, understanding, love from others and from oneself, as well as the gift of time used wisely. Along the way, the sensitive, healing heart acquires wisdom and compassion for fellow travelers.

Not all broken hearts inherit these gifts. They only come with intention, inner strength, persistence, courage and openness to the grace of God.

Be a life long or short, its completeness depends on what it was lived for.

David Starr Jordan

Joyce Harvey

Footnotes for Life

lmost every day I see a young girl running along our backcountry road. She is nothing but bone, her face classically anorexic: all cheekbones and large eyes sunk into dark sockets. I've watched her run for nine months now, seeing her grow thinner and more fragile every day. She is not like the other runners, all rounded muscle, strong, sweaty, solid. My girl is grim and solitary, a slash on the landscape. I wonder who her family is and know they cannot stop her self-punishment any more than I. She started running and stopped eating because she heard some wicked voice inside telling her she wasn't right, she wasn't thin enough. You will grow old if you're lucky, and being thin is no guarantee against misery.

The body never lies.

Martha Graham

Nancy Burke

Footnotes for Life

I never met my grandfather, however I did know his son and I knew that my father had very bitter feelings toward his father. According to the stories I heard, my grandfather drank himself to death at the age of fifty-two. During a breakfast outing with my five-year-old son my father looked at me and said, "Your grandfather sure wasn't much of a father." After a pause he let out a sigh and said, "But I guess the man did the best he could." Eight years into his own recovery and thirty-one years after the death of my grandfather, my dad had started to make peace with his father. Sometimes it takes a long time for things to heal.

Robert J. Ackerman

The greatest lesson to be learned is that the most difficult way is, in the long run, the easiest.

Henry Miller

Footnotes for Life

_____

_____

_____

_____

_____

_____

_____

_____

SEPTEMBER 14

Today I will ask for a miracle. I trust that nothing is more real in this universe than the love and the power of God. I understand that the medium of miracles and shifts in perception is prayer. I will clear my mind of all negativity and ask for what I really need. I will pray for a miracle. In the past I have not dared to ask for enough but today is different. With love in my heart I ask for a true shift in perception. I ask for help to see what I am not seeing, help to release the cloud of doubt and negativity that surrounds me, help to set my mind free of fear and anxiety.

The direction of the mind is more important than its progress.

Joseph Joubert

Tian Dayton

Footnotes for Life

_____

_____

_____

_____

_____

_____

_____

When I see the persistence exhibited by the tiny ant, as it builds its mound and drags along food it has found, I know the size of an obstacle has nothing to do with success.

It is not the physical proportion of an impediment, but the diligence we possess that gets us what we desire and the reward we receive.

Betty King

> *He is a man of sense who does not grieve for what he has not, but rejoices in what he has.*
>
> Epictetus

Footnotes for Life

_____

_____

_____

_____

_____

_____

_____

_____

SEPTEMBER 16

Although it may feel like I am alone, I am not. There is a circle of love around me. My circle includes neighbors, relatives, coworkers or those who are also recovering. If I reach out to these people I will feel their presence and concern.

I don't need to feel unworthy because I accept them with their imperfections and they do the same with me. My circle will help me recover if I ask.

Brenda Nixon

Let us not look back in anger or forward in fear, but around in awareness.

James Thurber

Footnotes for Life

_____

_____

_____

_____

_____

_____

_____

_____

SEPTEMBER 17

I give thanks for my life, knowing that all experiences have added to my growth and understanding. I see the promise of the future, anticipating only good. But today I center my attention on the present moment and look around my world. I see much in the way of good and much for which to give thanks. In all my activities I pause, I reflect, I give thanks. I look forward to happiness and opportunity and acknowledge the blessings surrounding me that are meant to be enjoyed now.

Rokelle Lerner

When asked if my cup is half full or half empty my only response is that I am thankful I have a cup.

Sam Lefkowitz

Footnotes for Life

_____

_____

_____

_____

_____

_____

_____

_____

SEPTEMBER 18

Some folks spend half their lives brooding about the past—chiding themselves for their mistakes and reliving in their minds, over and over again, what might have been. Others worry about the future—condemning their weaknesses and worrying that they will not be strong enough to overcome what may arise. But those of us in recovery strive to put the pain of our past and the fear of our future behind us. Rather, we find comfort and strength in the innocence of now, the present. With each new dawn we are reborn. And so we live . . . one day at a time.

Yesterday is history, tomorrow is a mystery, and today is a gift: that's why they call it the present.

Eleanor Roosevelt

Kay Conner Pliszka

Footnotes for Life

I see the full picture of recovery and my responsibility to let go and move on. Doing so is a tall order, requiring a kind of releasing that I still find difficult to do. My past will always be in the shadows of my memory to haunt me if I do not recognize it as a part of me. If I pretend it's not important, grit my teeth and force myself to numb the pain, I have missed the point of recovery. On the other hand, if I am unwilling to let go, I am not allowing myself to be fully healthy and alive. Part of recovery is a flowing through the stored pain and part is a decisive, forward-moving action.

Tian Dayton

Our concern is not how to worship in the catacombs but how to remain human in the skyscrapers.

Abraham Joshua Heschel

Footnotes for Life

_____

_____

_____

_____

_____

_____

_____

_____

SEPTEMBER 20

Everyone has problems and it's easy to get overwhelmed, thinking there is no solution. Small steps can make a big difference. Today, instead of thinking about what I can't do, I'll think about what I can do to solve the problem. Whether something is wrong in my personal life, my work life, my neighborhood, my community or the world—I can make a difference. If I continue to focus on and do what I can do, I find that what I thought was impossible suddenly becomes doable.

Sarah White

Nothing in the world can take the place of persistence.

Calvin Coolidge

Footnotes for Life

_____

_____

_____

_____

_____

_____

_____

SEPTEMBER 21

God graces us with personal power to make unlimited choices. This amazing capacity can positively transform our lives when we reserve it for healthy decisions. Respect the gift of power in your life. Recognize that it is bestowed with a significant expectation: Responsibility.

Linda Suroviec

> *No individual raindrop considers itself responsible for the flood.*
>
> Unknown

Footnotes for Life

A new normal . . . each day is a new "normal" for me as I progress in my recovery. The challenge is to see the progress—recognize the positive movement no matter how small—and celebrate it. In the end, my "normal" may never be what it was before the day, the event, that forever changed my life. But, I will celebrate the fact that there *is* another day. And, I am a stronger person because of my challenge, my progress and my attitude. A new normal. A better me.

Charmi Schroeder

When we move out of the familiar here and now, we set in motion a series of events that, taken together, bring about changes at the very root of our being.

Joseph Dispenza

Footnotes for Life

_____

_____

_____

_____

_____

_____

_____

I walk through this day because of you, Lord. No personal power of my own gets me out of bed and onto my knees. By your strength, I walk. By your grace, I keep going. When I stumble, you catch me in your arms, and when I fall, you carry me. You hold my breath in your hands and you understand all of my ways. Because of you, I can flee from self pity, and I am thankful beyond words, just to be alive!

Jaye Lewis

I have taken a moment here to rest, to steal a view of the glorious vista that surrounds me, to look back on the distance I have come.

Nelson Mandela

Footnotes for Life

_____

_____

_____

_____

_____

_____

_____

_____

SEPTEMBER 24

Like a time traveler from a science fiction movie, I bumped into myself the other day. I shouldn't say myself because the self I encountered in an old journal hasn't been around for decades. As I fingered the crinkly pages of loose-leaf notebook paper, deeply scored by the anxious tip of a ballpoint pen, I felt as though I'd stepped into another time and place. I read the strangely familiar writing, more rounded and innocent than I remembered, wondering whether I had really been so naïve. So idealistic. So noble. My old journal brought me face-to-face with myself and taught me that I was worth knowing.

Eleanor Kirk

> *Man does not weave this web of life. He is merely a strand of it. Whatever he does to the web, he does to himself.*
>
> Chief Seattle

Footnotes for Life

In my journey I have purpose on Earth and I will continue to strengthen my direction. When I get confused and flounder around, searching for my bearings, I take time to remind myself that my Higher Power is guiding my journey and I feel tranquil and at peace. Growing up in a dysfunctional family, my energies were blocked by my inability to separate from the emotions of others. When the alcoholic was drinking, I felt uptight, fearful and filled with anxiety. Today, I don't live in extremes. I have purpose. Being alive is a miracle to celebrate and I feel the harmony that comes when I channel my energy into good directions.

Find a purpose in life so big it will challenge every capacity to be at your best.

David O. McKay

Rokelle Lerner

Footnotes for Life

_____

_____

_____

_____

_____

_____

_____

_____

SEPTEMBER 26

We learn in recovery that the definition of insanity is doing the same thing over and over again and expecting different results. Many times I swore that I would only have two drinks at a party only to wake up with a horrific hangover. With no memory of how I'd gotten home, I would try to piece the evening together and I would promise myself, *never again!* But then came the next party and my promises flew out of my head as quickly as you can say "punch bowl." Mine was a soul sickness whose name is Alcoholism. I have learned to swallow my medicine—I gratefully attend A.A. meetings now. When the urge to say "yes" hits I remember that no drink will ever taste as good as my sober dignity feels.

We choose our joys and sorrows long before we experience them.

Kahlil Gibran

Dorri Olds

Footnotes for Life

_____

_____

_____

_____

_____

_____

_____

_____

As I stand behind the Plexiglas at the rink watching my son on the ice, I recall a doctor's visit when Paul was three. Paul couldn't talk, had terrible tantrums, always kept to himself. He had autism. That dark day I felt like we had been pushed off a cliff, but instead of a living death we found miracles. Angels in the form of teachers, therapists and childcare workers intervened, some of whom I would never have chosen if I had done the choosing. I gladly admit I was wrong. God, who knows the end from the beginning, knew what Paul needed in his challenging journey and that I needed to learn a lesson in faith and letting go.

Mistakes are the portals of discovery.

James Joyce

Jayne Thurber-Smith

Footnotes for Life

SEPTEMBER 28

I searched for a way to pour out my heartache and sorrow, struggling to find comfort and solace after the death of my four-year-old son. I needed a friend, non-judgmental, who would never tell a soul what I had shared. Feeling like a bottle capped too tightly I needed to unwind, to release some of my pain. My search brought me to pen and paper, to the pages of a safe book—my journal—where I experienced the healing in writing to recover. For eight years I have filled the pages and what began as pain and undeniable anger now reads as sweet joy.

Alice J. Wisler

Children are innocent and love justice, while most adults are wicked and prefer mercy.

G.K. Chesterton

Footnotes for Life

Once you've been sober a while you realize that sobriety is not just about putting down your addiction. That's only the beginning. Sobriety is about letting the light of the spirit shine through, and letting you be the person you were always meant to be. Putting down the addiction is like scrubbing long-dirty windows, what you finally see behind the glass has been there all the time, you just never saw how beautiful it was.

Kelly L. Stone

If one advances confidently in the direction of his dreams and endeavors to live the life which he has imagined, he will meet with a success unexpected in common hours.

Henry David Thoreau

Footnotes for Life

_____

_____

_____

_____

_____

_____

_____

_____

When I look in the mirror today, let me see beyond the obvious. Beyond the tired eyes, let me see strength I didn't know I had. Past the lines on my face, let me see character that wasn't there before. Let me see someone who has grown and changed and will continue to do so. Someone who is a little bit stronger, a little bit wiser and a little bit better than yesterday. When I look at myself, let me see not only what's there . . . but what else is there.

Lori Othouse

*There are no shortcuts
to any place
worth going.*

Beverly Sills

Footnotes for Life

_____

_____

_____

_____

_____

_____

_____

Life does not pass me by—I pass through it. There are stars to count, flowers to touch, people to greet, fragrances to enjoy, sounds to hear. I am alive.

Today I will take an active role in the quality of life all around me. Intention and action are my reality.

Brenda Nixon

> *Life is like playing a violin solo in public and learning the instrument as one goes on.*
>
> Samuel Butler

Footnotes for Life

_____

_____

_____

_____

_____

_____

_____

_____

OCTOBER 2

The dance of life has simple moves. Follow your heart. Lead with your soul. Be true to yourself. Find what sparks your soul and kindles your inner fire.

When disappointments bring on ominous skies and threatening storms, embrace your dreams. Your dreams are those warm rays of hope that will keep you anchored until the sun shines tomorrow.

Know that soon you will whirl and waltz with the wind again.

Maryellen Heller

If you're already walking on thin ice, you might as well dance.

Gill Atkinson

Footnotes for Life

_____

_____

_____

_____

_____

_____

_____

A humble person dismisses nothing, recognizing that whatever life presents needs to be respected. Inside even the smallest things there is often enormity. Being humble does not require you to give of yourself indiscriminately. Have the wisdom to know the value of your inner resources and to give accordingly.

Brahma Kumaris
World Spiritual University

By maintaining an attitude of love and regard for every soul, you create a life filled with dignity and purpose.

Brahma Kumaris

Footnotes for Life

_____

_____

_____

_____

_____

_____

_____

_____

OCTOBER 4

Today I will surround myself with people who care about me. I take deep satisfaction in knowing there are people in my life I can turn to. I, too, can be a friend. I can give support and nurturing to others without becoming responsible for their lives. In the past, I avoided friendships because they became too painful, too demanding. I expected too much of myself and I expected too much of others. I now realize that I no longer need to isolate myself from friendship. I cannot solve the problems of my friends, and they cannot solve mine. But we can give each other support, we can listen, we can care for each other. Friendship and recovery go hand in hand.

A true friend never gets in your way unless you happen to be going down.

Arnold Glasgow

Rokelle Lerner

Footnotes for Life

Your recovering journey may require some U-turns along the way, but there is a plan, a destiny that awaits you.

Do not question your destiny, do not ask "why me?" Be proud of who you are, walk with courage and your head up high. Believe in yourself and focus on the positive, for every step along the way will become a solid foundation for your future.

Stacey Chillemi

Confidence is that feeling by which the mind embarks on great and honorable courses with a sure hope and trust in itself.

Cicero

Footnotes for Life

_____

_____

_____

_____

_____

_____

_____

_____

OCTOBER 6

I am not alone. Today I will remember there are others facing the same hurdles and struggles I am facing. Others understand and feel the same pain I feel. There are available means and people that care about my recovery, and want to see me heal. I can reach out to others. I am not my own island. I want to seek opportunities for connection. I can break the silence and tell someone trustworthy. That will make me feel better!

Kimberly Davidson

I was never less alone than when by myself.

Edward Gibbon

Footnotes for Life

As you navigate through life, there will be times when you will feel overwhelmed. When you do, it is important to take a step back and assess the situation, try to view it from another perspective.

The obstacles in your life will enable you to grow into the person you are meant to become.

Karen Marie Arel

Today, I can choose to celebrate what I do have—or mourn what I don't. I choose to make today a celebration.

Charmi Schroeder

Footnotes for Life

_____

_____

_____

_____

_____

_____

_____

_____

OCTOBER 8

Going through my trunk one day, I stopped to read and memories of my life appeared, blessing me again.

I lingered on some photos of those no longer here. I thanked God for the time with many held so dear. I found my granddad's Bible, its pages old and torn. My name is written in that book on the day that I was born.

Good memories are precious photos upon our hearts.

Joan Clayton

I closed the trunk remembering our lives are short at best. Fill your trunk with goodness and God will do the rest.

Joan Clayton

Footnotes for Life

OCTOBER 9

In every journey there can be meaning; every conflict, growth; in every action, there can be purpose but only if I allow it to be so.

I will look at my mistakes as learning what works and what doesn't.

Today, I will allow meaning, growth, purpose and learning in my life.

Brenda Nixon

Be not afraid of growing slowly; be afraid only of standing still.

Chinese Proverb

Footnotes for Life

_____

_____

_____

_____

_____

_____

_____

_____

My son's drug rehabilitation counselor was a petite grey-haired lady with enough leverage to impact a wayward group of teens. Her personal struggle with alcohol and drugs was the source of a spirit of determination, and week after week her motto, "You gotta wanna!", spewed from her lips. The powerful testimony of an achiever made a difference in my son's life and over the years, whenever I find myself in a situation that takes strong will and determination, I hear those words "You gotta wanna!", echoing like a voice of victory in my ears.

Annettee Budzban

Great beginnings are not as important as the way one finishes.

Dr. James Dobson

Footnotes for Life

_____

_____

_____

_____

_____

_____

_____

_____

OCTOBER 11

Every day is a new page; the words are up to you. Will the page be filled with "if only . . ." or with "I did it!"? When your life winds down will you be wallowing in your regrets or celebrating your experiences and accomplishments? When you share that book of memories, will there be a smile on your face as you relive your journey or a tear in your eye for the missed opportunities and the what might have been? It is your choice, tomorrow is a new day, turn the page and write your life the way you want it to be. You do not always travel the path of your choosing; sometimes it is the path you were meant to take.

I find the great thing in this world is not so much where we stand, as in what direction we are moving.

Oliver Wendell Holmes

Karen Marie Arel

Footnotes for Life

_____

_____

_____

_____

_____

_____

_____

_____

OCTOBER 12

Healing demands energy. To sustain my energy I will remember that in my loving of and giving to others, I must keep a little for myself. It's good to give but not so much that I am emptied. The healthy balance between giving and keeping is important for my recovery.

Today, I can give to others and I can also be my caretaker.

Fond as we are of our loved ones, there comes at times during their absence an unexplainable peace.

Anne Shaw

I will not feel guilty for loving and giving to myself, as this is the energy needed for recovery.

Brenda Nixon

Footnotes for Life

_____

_____

_____

_____

_____

_____

_____

_____

Like many others who have found themselves in trouble, I returned to the church of my childhood when things seemed their darkest. At our Thanksgiving Mass this year, a day we hold as sacred as any other holy day, there was a moment in the liturgy when we stood, held hands and said the Lord's Prayer together. I held the hand of my eight-year-old, who held the hand of an eighty-year-old, and the circle moved on, hand-over-hand, unbroken, among the five hundred in church. The presence of God was indisputable, the power of faith breathtaking. In our collective gratitude, we all became, at the moment, immortal.

Nancy Burke

The body is a universe in itself and must be held as sacred as any thing in creation. It is dangerous to forget the body is sacramental.

May Sarton

Footnotes for Life

_____

_____

_____

_____

_____

_____

_____

_____

OCTOBER 14

In days past, it seemed that everything she touched died. But she tended a little herb garden. At least there she could make things live . . . except for the lemon balm. Year after year, it grew well for a while and then died. It was a little thing, only one plant out of many, but it had become symbolic of all her failures. She finally gave up. Years later, she watched curiously as a tiny plant that was obviously not a weed emerged from the soil. When the leaves grew large enough, she pinched them gently and sniffed. It was a baby lemon balm! Sometimes seeds hibernate. Be patient. They are only waiting for the right time to emerge.

Rhonda Brunea

Don't judge each day by the harvest you reap, but by the seeds you plant.

Robert Louis Stevenson

Footnotes for Life

I was thirty-eight years old before I understood that no matter what I did or said, my mother and father could not parent any better than they had. It was beyond their ability and more important, was nothing personal. One of the most precious gifts of my recovery was accepting that my mom and dad just didn't possess boundless love, endless nurturing, playfulness, tenderness or fun to give. I was lucky enough and had the courage to find a way to let go of my idealized vision of what my parents' love should look like. Before they passed away, the expressions of love that had started out as unilateral behaviors on my part became mutual.

> *It is a wise father who knows his own child.*
>
> William Shakespeare

Ted Klontz

Footnotes for Life

_____

_____

_____

_____

_____

_____

_____

_____

OCTOBER 16

Before recovery I didn't understand choices; I didn't realize I actually had them. I spent my life reacting to situations I believed were out of my control.

Now my life is based on choices; I choose how I think, and my thoughts create my reality. I choose how to respond, or not to respond. I move forward, learn to live with my choice, or change my direction.

Deb Sellars Karpek

Right now you are one choice away from a new beginning.

Oprah Winfrey

Footnotes for Life

_____

_____

_____

_____

_____

_____

_____

My dad once said, "Everybody has a string pulled a little too tight." He drew a circle and from the center he drew rays to represent taut strings. One line he labeled VANITY, another GREED; the next, LUST, etc.

I guess Dad was trying to say that nobody is perfect and that, on some level, each of us has a weakness that makes us a bit "nutty." But we learn and we grow. And if, in the challenges of each day, we persevere and hold firm to our beliefs and our goals, we will flourish.

Today's mighty oak is just yesterday's nut that held its ground.

Unknown

Kay Conner Pliszka

Footnotes for Life

_____

_____

_____

_____

_____

_____

_____

_____

OCTOBER 18

You never truly stop being beautiful. Your age creates a glow of wisdom and confidence that silvers your hair and puts a step of grace into your walk.

You shine as your true self, the one that took the years to perfect.

Nadia Ali

The truly important things in life—love, beauty, and one's own uniqueness—are constantly being overlooked.

Pablo Casals

Footnotes for Life

_____

_____

_____

_____

_____

_____

_____

In times of great trial, we often find ourselves not knowing what to do, or which way to turn. In the midst of confusion, it's easy to block out the needs of those around us, choosing to inwardly focus on our own misery. However, reaching out to others helps us regain balance in our lives. In redirecting our energy toward easing another's burdens, our own burdens not only become lighter, but we find reasons to rejoice . . . newly blessed by all we've been given. In walking a mile in the other man's shoes, we have an opportunity to gain new appreciation for the perfect fit of our own.

We must learn our limits. We are all something, but none of us are everything.

Blaise Pascal

Michelle Close-Mills

Footnotes for Life

_____

_____

_____

_____

_____

_____

_____

_____

The fragility or strength of the motivating force behind your will determines the success of dreams and the distance they travel. As we live our lives we run into successes or failures; our choosing makes the difference in the two.

Ideas originate in the hallowed hallways of the mind, from feelings and beliefs, and are spurred on into the heart where they meet up with will and determination, or die from apprehension. It is when the soul grabs hold of dreams and refuses to release them until they see fruition, that a person truly knows the joy that imaginings can bring.

Betty King

What I can imagine, I can see. What I can see, I can grab hold of, what I can grab hold of is mine.

Betty King

Footnotes for Life

_____

_____

_____

_____

_____

_____

_____

_____

OCTOBER 21

Recovery takes time. If I am impatient with my healing I cheat myself of the necessary time it takes to go through my own grief. To pretend that I have never experienced real despair is to sabotage myself, to become complicit in emotional dishonesty. I know I have the strength I need to get through my pain and part of my strength is not ignoring my emotions. I entrust myself to God with a sure knowledge that my healing is now taking place.

Rokelle Lerner

Health is not a condition of matter, but of mind.

Mary Baker Eddy

Footnotes for Life

_____

_____

_____

_____

_____

_____

_____

_____

OCTOBER 22

In our culture, we emphasize the body, exalt the intellect and worship talent. Yet, the flesh is just the package, the wrapping paper for the true prize—our spirit. Life leaves the bows and ribbons a bit frayed and the brightly colored paper fades with time, but through difficulties our spirit grows. The spirit shapes our true destiny. It is the spirit that makes each one of us intrinsically priceless and eternally precious.

Renee Hixson

Faith is a knowledge within the heart, beyond the reach of proof.

Kahlil Gibran

Footnotes for Life

I know that I can do anything I need to do with God's help. When I feel alone or shaken up, I can ask for help within myself and know that it is there. Each of us has to learn our own lessons, that is what we are here to do. We can't learn anyone else's lessons for them and learning our own is difficult enough. To plow through my own psyche and face the insecurity and wounds that are there is all that I can handle. To try to live other people's lives for them is to separate myself from God because my first access to God is through and within me.

Tian Dayton

One on God's side is a majority.

Wendell Phillips

Footnotes for Life

_____

_____

_____

_____

_____

_____

_____

_____

OCTOBER 24

It feels wonderful to love someone else and to have someone love you, but there's nothing more wonderful than loving who you are. Allow yourself to see your inner beauty, your strengths and how much you have to offer this world. You are special and unique; you brighten the lives of others. Take the energy and passion you put into loving others, and direct it to loving who you are.

Cori Sachais Swidorsky

I pay no attention whatever to anybody's praise or blame. I simply follow my own feelings.

Wolfgang Amadeus Mozart

Footnotes for Life

_____

_____

_____

_____

_____

_____

_____

I have a little booklet my grandfather wrote. He speaks to me through words on a yellowed page and I hear the voice of a man I have never met. Sometimes I think he left the stories especially for me, although for him I was only a prediction. I come from a long line of storytellers—their wares passed from one generation to the next in the fashion of heirlooms. Like any inheritance the value lies with the recipient. I hold the stories passed to me close to my heart. My mother used to tell me that I was the promise her father made—the baby sent to her after his passing. At fifty years old I still love that story.

Elva Stoelers

Your scars are evidence that you have healed.

Dr. Julia Boyd

Footnotes for Life

_____

_____

_____

_____

_____

_____

_____

_____

OCTOBER 26

Sometimes indulging yourself is the best answer to feeling wonderful. Cook something that is simply delicious that takes a lot of effort! Something you would make for company.

Today you are making it just for yourself, so don't rush through the process.

Then when it's done, set the table beautifully. Use candles. Use your best dishes. And one beautiful rose in a bud vase. You are celebrating yourself. Enjoy!

Felice Prager

Without haste,
but without rest.

Goethe

Footnotes for Life

_____

_____

_____

_____

_____

_____

_____

OCTOBER 27

Living a life of honesty is a commitment to forthright thinking and behavior—a willingness to be fully responsible. Honesty enables me to live with an open heart and to avoid the self-loathing, guilt and shame that accompany deception and manipulation. Perhaps most significantly, it is an outward display of self-acceptance and a statement to the world that I am worthy of respect.

Jeff McFarland

No legacy is so rich as honesty.

William Shakespeare

Footnotes for Life

OCTOBER 28

D iamonds are nothing special, really. They started out as simple chunks of coal. They just got a lot of preferential treatment—and not the kind they would have chosen. They became diamonds because they were put under enough heat and pressure to crystallize. No pressure, no diamonds. We are diamonds in the making. Let us persist under pressure.

Barbara A. Croce

Diamonds are nothing more than chunks of coal that stuck to their jobs.

Malcolm S. Forbes

Footnotes for Life

_____

_____

_____

_____

_____

_____

_____

Today I will learn to see soul in the simple things of life. It is oftentimes the things that I take for granted that are truly responsible for the deep underpinnings of my sense of well-being and personal happiness. When I let myself have and enjoy events of life, I will see soul radiate from the simple and the little things.

Life is a tapestry woven of small threads. I appreciate what I take for granted.

Tian Dayton

> *When you see ordinary situations with extraordinary insight, it is like discovering a jewel in rubbish.*
>
> Chögyan Trungpa

Footnotes for Life

OCTOBER 30

Growing up in an alcoholic home, crisis was common and made life confusing. Feelings of anxiety and fear were my constant companions. Crisis is no longer a condition I live with. I do whatever I can to ensure my serenity and my peace of mind. I allow enough time for myself to do what I need. I eliminate clutter from my life and shun discord and over-complication. I think before I act, I'm kind to myself and I avoid situations filled with pandemonium and turmoil. Slow down and let serenity flow into your life.

Rokelle Lerner

A person needs at intervals to separate from family and companions and go to new places. One must go without familiars in order to be open to influences, to change.

Katharine Butler Hathaway

Footnotes for Life

_____

_____

_____

_____

_____

_____

_____

OCTOBER 31

It is difficult to pretend to be happy when I am not. The hurt and anger lingers as I try to recover from the pain of loss. As I try to drink my hurt away, I reach for the wine bottle from the cabinet in my kitchen. Just as I move my hand away from the top shelf, my Bible topples down and lands on my kitchen table. A reminder, what would be more refreshing, a temporary cure or lasting tranquility and inner peace. I have replaced my drinking hour with my thinking hour. I devote some time each morning for inspirational reading and thought as I learn to take one day at a time.

Theresa Meehan

Every trial endured and weathered in the right spirit makes a soul nobler and stronger than it was before.

James Buckham

Footnotes for Life

Newly sober, Grace quickly returned to a high-risk environment working as a flight attendant. One day she was hit with an overwhelming desire for a drink. She tried to just "think through" or "forget about" it, but it was too powerful and she headed for the airport bar. Deep down inside she really wanted to stay sober and in a moment of sanity she picked up the airport page and said "Will friends of Bill W. . . .," she paused quickly looking for an empty gate, ". . . please come to Gate 12?" Within minutes strangers from all over the world joined Grace for a little meeting. Grace did not drink that day. Help is there for all who ask. It never fails.

Begin somewhere; you cannot build a reputation on what you intend to do.

Liz Smith

Jim C., Jr., Scottsdale, Arizona

Footnotes for Life

NOVEMBER 2

When I enter into a relationship with the idea that another person can make me happy and content, I become concerned over what I might or might not get back. If I relieve others from the responsibility for making me happy, I can enjoy intimate relationships based upon mutual caring, not on need. I deserve a relationship, not to make me happy, but to share the richness of who I am with others.

Rokelle Lerner

Always do what you say you are going to do. It is the glue and fiber that binds successful relationships.

Jeffrey A. Timmons

Footnotes for Life

Life is a glorious mystery. After we have understood one thing, we are presented with a fresh problem. We are not perfect. We are not God. We will never understand completely. Some years ago this used to anger and irritate me. I wanted to know everything. I wanted to have the answer to all life's problems. I wanted the "power" that comes with perfection. I hated being vulnerable, weak and confused! I hated being human! Yes, that was my problem. I hated being a human being. Today I am enjoying the adventure of life, and I kneel in awe at its mingled complexity. Today life is a paradox that I can live with.

Father Leo Booth

> *The future is hidden even from the men who made it.*
>
> Anatole France

Footnotes for Life

_____

_____

_____

_____

_____

_____

_____

_____

NOVEMBER 4

When faced with tossing a few bucks into the jar of an unfortunate soul I wonder if by doing so I'm supporting a person's addiction or falling victim to a scam. I usually decide that for the price of a scratch ticket, I'd rather give a person the benefit of the doubt. With thousands swallowed up by substance abuse, alcoholism, unemployment and homelessness each day, it could easily be me or someone I love walking in those worn shoes. The next time you ask yourself why God has given so much to so few, and so little to so many, consider this: perhaps God has given enough and the problem is that people have forgotten how to share his generous gifts.

More people would learn from their mistakes if they weren't so busy denying them.

Unknown

Steven Manchester

Footnotes for Life

A rainy day can get me feeling down. The gray skies, the dull colors, the dripping rain. I see and hear this and my spirit sags. Occasionally, responding this way sets me on a downward spiral of feeling even worse, because I expect myself to be cheery and positive. The self judge comes alive with, "Why am I letting a little rain get me down?" My body can be very sensitive to changes in the environment and knowing that can help me ease up on judging myself. I can't always be upbeat and happy in the same way that it can't always be sunny and bright, however I can always allow myself to be with every mood I feel.

Anne Conner

She said she usually cried at least once each day, not because she was sad, but because the world was so beautiful . . . and life was so short.

Brian Andreas

Footnotes for Life

NOVEMBER 6

When you are in the grips of a compulsion to act on an addictive behavior, be kind to yourself; stop, breathe and, above all, remember the feeling will pass.

Reach out to supportive friends, go for a walk or see a movie and wait; one minute, one hour, one day—until the agony and temptation pass leaving strength, determination and pride in their place.

Lisa Jo Barr

Be very careful, then, how you live, not as unwise but as wise, making the most of every opportunity.

Ephesians 5:15,16 NIV

Footnotes for Life

_____

_____

_____

_____

_____

_____

_____

Everything needed for our happiness and serenity already lies within. Problem is, it's often buried deeply beneath the lies, prejudices, chaos and traumas that we experience or are taught. Life's challenge, your challenge, my challenge, is to avoid the search for happiness or serenity through external or chemical means. Rather, we must commit to passionately and to consciously find the kingdom of heaven within us, sifting through the debris, finding the best parts of our inner selves, finding that which connects us spiritually, and bringing that inner self to life.

There is always a certain peace in being what one is, in being that completely.

Ugo Betti

Kevin J. Holmes

Footnotes for Life

_____

_____

_____

_____

_____

_____

_____

_____

I search for silver linings, for the deeper meaning of events in my life. When I feel pain or confusion, when I am discouraged or hurting, I look for the hand of spirit in my life. I try to understand what I am meant to see that I am not seeing, what I am meant to hear that I am not hearing. My life is a journey and I cannot stay on my path of spiritual development if I am not willing to experience the truth of my inner world. I can grow in joy and pain. It doesn't need to be one or the other because pain can transform into joy. It can be the fire that clears the field for new and tender growth.

Tian Dayton

Whatever you can do or dream you can begin it. Boldness has genius, power and magic in it. Begin it now.

Goethe

Footnotes for Life

_____

_____

_____

_____

_____

_____

_____

I was cleaning out my files when I came across some things I had written during my darkest hours. The writing was full of pain and anger. I felt for that woman, for the horrible things she had been through. Tears rolled down my face as I looked into the black hole where I used to live. My first instinct was to throw the pages of despair into the trash, then I realized that this is what all the work had been for. Everything I had been through had allowed me to move outside the hopelessness to a place where I could recognize the light.

Anne Tiller Slates

The life of every man is a diary and his humblest hour is when he compares the volume as it is with what he vowed to make it.

James M. Barrie

Footnotes for Life

_____

_____

_____

_____

_____

_____

_____

_____

NOVEMBER 10

Time is the currency of our lives. We get another stash of it every morning. We trade it for what we want or need, or we waste it—it's really up to us. But one thing is for sure: we can't save time for tomorrow. We have to use it up today. It won't wait for us. If we do not spend it on purpose, it'll disburse itself, one second at a time. It runs out at midnight.

Barbara A. Croce

Life is meant to be a celebration! It shouldn't be necessary to set aside special times to remind us of this fact.

Leo Buscaglia

Footnotes for Life

_____

_____

_____

_____

_____

_____

_____

_____

NOVEMBER 11

Driver's license suspended, I did what any normal person would do. I bought a horse and I rode him every night to my hangouts. Morning would find the horse out back and me in my own bed with no recollection of how we had gotten home. Years later a newcomer in the rooms told us about a young man arriving at her bar drunk on a horse. "I wonder what ever happened to that guy?" she mused. To the amusement of the rest of the group, I took the opportunity to properly introduce myself. I am often asked why I still attend meetings after so many years of sobriety. The answer: my presence might help the newcomer.

Reverend Bob Lew

> *Man is condemned to be free; because once thrown into the world, he is responsible for everything he does.*
>
> Jean-Paul Sartre

Footnotes for Life

_____

_____

_____

_____

_____

_____

_____

_____

A winter landscape can be cold, hard and bleak. The ground is unyielding and barren, devoid of vegetation and hungry for the sun's warming touch. There is no sign of spring, and you wonder if it will ever come. The tulips of March and the daffodils of April are nothing but a hazy dream.

Life can feel like that. You become lonely and hardened because of attacks and defeats. You step back from relationships and avoid challenges. It is easier to isolate yourself than to be vulnerable once more. And then, out of the hard, snow-covered ground, when it is least expected, a crocus blooms.

Ava Pennington

Have patience with all things, but first of all with yourself.

St. Francis de Sales

Footnotes for Life

_____

_____

_____

_____

_____

_____

_____

I will not insist upon perfection from myself in order to feel good. Why should each thing I do have to be excellent in my eyes, or someone else's, in order for me to feel happy with it? The idea is that I enjoy the process, that what I do feels satisfying and interesting. Being addicted to success every time means that eventually I will dry up my own creative source because success every time is not natural. When I allow myself to enjoy and experience satisfaction with whatever I am doing, I keep the doors open for my own creative flow. When I do not accept what I do unless it's just right, I close off my own inner flow.

Tian Dayton

> *I think I did pretty well, considering I started out with nothing but a bunch of blank paper.*
>
> Steve Martin

Footnotes for Life

NOVEMBER 14

It is by experiencing something's opposite that we come to know the thing itself. Fearful, we find faith; a victim, we become empowered. Knowing lack, we understand abundance. Being stuck, we can embrace flow. Enduring pain, we can embody joy. Because we have hated, we can know love. In flirting with insanity, we can understand clarity. Having locked ourselves in a mental prison, we can know freedom. As we peer over the ledge of death, we can truly embody life. To the exact degree that we have cut ourselves off from the divine, infinite flow of God, we can now recognize its presence.

Jeffrey R. Anderson

God gives every bird his worm, but he does not throw it into the nest.

Swedish Proverb

Footnotes for Life

_____

_____

_____

_____

_____

_____

_____

What is the difference between maintaining sobriety and living a life in recovery? Staying sober often means just hanging on with white knuckles or facing the day with clenched teeth. Recovery brings heartfelt gratitude and joy to life. Both require a commitment to yourself and both are based on choices. Sobriety is a choice to avoid the negative behaviors that draw you back to the old ways of living and thinking. Recovery is a choice to incorporate positive behaviors into your life that allow you to move toward health and well-being, physically and spiritually.

> *Things do not change, we change.*
>
> Henry David Thoreau

Joyce McDonald Hoskins

Footnotes for Life

_____

_____

_____

_____

_____

_____

_____

_____

NOVEMBER 16

When you believe you've committed an offense, do not berate yourself or your mistake will be compounded. Instead, offer prompt amends, correct your awareness for the future and move the experience into your past. Remember, even at our very best we will never surpass being human. Accept the fact that recovery does not prevent you from making mistakes, it merely provides the tools you'll need to fix the things that need mending.

Lisa Logan

He who keeps his face towards the sun, will find that the shadows fall behind him.

Native American Saying

Footnotes for Life

NOVEMBER 17

I am sorting out my relationships with a new awareness, with a new vision of what I desire in an intimate relationship and I am slowly making the changes necessary to get what I want. In my alcoholic home, intimacy was confused with smothering or caretaking. In my adult life, I have isolated myself for periods of time to avoid it. My notions about what it means to be close to another human being are being redefined. I'm beginning to understand that I don't have to be responsible for someone to show my love for them, nor do I have to give up my identity in order to achieve intimacy. Allowing the ones I love to be human means I can search for happiness not perfection.

Love demands infinitely less than friendship.

George Jean Nathan

Rokelle Lerner

Footnotes for Life

It is heroic to feed a starving village and noble to give water to a thirsty man who is about to perish. Yet, when someone is obnoxious, irritating and generally unpleasant we stay away. Their chosen demeanor isolates them, deepening the loneliness that reinforces their unpleasant personality. Such a person is starving and thirsting for love, dying for the very commodity we withhold. To reach past the thorns and touch such a soul is an act of true compassion. This is what changes the world.

Renee Hixson

To be hopeful in bad times is not just foolishly romantic. It is based on the fact that human history is a history not only of cruelty but also of compassion, sacrifice, courage, kindness.

Howard Zinn

Footnotes for Life

I will pay attention to the contents of my thoughts. Even when I do not give voice to them, others feel them as nonverbal messages. What I think is more powerful than I care to admit. The thoughts I think exist in living tissue and move through and beyond me. They become a part of the creative substance of life. They take a shape, they have an impact. I see myself as a traveler moving through the world knowing I am not here forever. I am here to experience where I am. I will observe my thoughts and my actions and see how they affect my life.

Tian Dayton

We cannot withdraw our cards from the game. Were we as silent and as mute as stories, our very passivity would be an act.

Jean-Paul Sartre

Footnotes for Life

_____

_____

_____

_____

_____

_____

_____

_____

Emergency room personnel transported the dirty outsider to the sterile world of the cardiac care unit. Thick, scaly, ruddy skin told a story of an abusive lifestyle, punctuated by addictive behavior to food, alcohol and drugs. As his nurse began to bathe him she prayed for the soul of a little boy grown up, rejected by life and striving for acceptance in a hostile world. She finished with warmed lotion and baby powder, such a contrast on the huge, rugged surface. As he rolled over onto his back, tears fell from beautiful brown eyes and a quivering voice whispered, "Thank you." In this hurting world, with its concern about the appropriateness of touch, dare to touch the untouchable.

When love and skill work together, expect a masterpiece.

John Ruskin

Naomi Rhode

Footnotes for Life

When we are truly ready to surrender—after weeks or months or years of pining half-heartedly for that something greater than ourselves, that intangible power that has always seemed just beyond reach—we find the faith to fall into the arms of hope and love that have been there all the while.

Candy Killion

There is no need to go to India or anywhere else to find peace. You will find that deep place of silence right in your room, your garden, or even your bathtub.

Elisabeth Kübler-Ross

Footnotes for Life

_____

_____

_____

_____

_____

_____

_____

_____

Every so often, the enormity and complexity of my work gives me the impression that there is little I can really do to help people. I become frustrated and overwhelmed with the problems of others. And with this powerlessness, I may become controlling. As a helper, I am a catalyst. It isn't my job to provide others with "the answers," rather I can be a powerful change agent, providing others with opportunities to discover their own solutions. I believe in the inherent beauty and strength in all human beings, and I will not assume that I know what's best for everyone. Instead I will model decisiveness, strength, security and inner peace that will reverberate to those around me.

The first step towards the solution of any problem is optimism.

John Baines

Rokelle Lerner

Footnotes for Life

Some things eat away at us, nibbling like mice on Swiss cheese. And, if we allow it to continue, we risk winding up as nothing more than holes. Revenge is one of those things. A canker. A corrosive. A corrupter of our souls. Entertaining thoughts of vengeance can satisfy our taste for spite, at least for the moment. But, in the end, it is, quite simply, exhausting. It prevents us from healing and moving on. How much wiser of us to recognize that the only people we need to get even with—to pay back—are those who seek only to help us.

Carol McAdoo Rehme

Do not let the hero in your soul perish in lonely frustration for the life you deserved, but have never been able to reach.

Ayn Rand

Footnotes for Life

_____

_____

_____

_____

_____

_____

_____

_____

Real recovery has little to do with what the path that we walk looks like—where we live, what we drive, how much money we have—but everything to do with how we choose to walk our life path.

It is our perspective, our attitude and our choices that transform us into who we are, that make our life experience what it is. We get to choose. Real recovery means learning to look at life in ways we never have before.

Jeffrey R. Anderson

Life is like an echo. We get from it what we put into it and, just like an echo, it often gives us much more.

Boris Lauer-Leonardi

Footnotes for Life

_____

_____

_____

_____

_____

_____

_____

I t is easy to confuse greatness of character with strength and brawn. Greatness of character, however, is usually best defined in the grace of inability or dependency. It is in the humbleness in asking for help without being forced through defeat to do it. Greatness of character is when you know that weakness is momentary and it ends when it seeks the strength of another.

Michelle Gipson

Discover something about yourself that will make you great: your weaknesses.

Michelle Gipson

Footnotes for Life

_____

_____

_____

_____

_____

_____

_____

_____

The bird doesn't know he flys. He has no "faith" in his wings. What he has is a lifetime of little experiences in which, when he feels the edge of the earth disappear and sees nothing but emptiness beneath his feet, still he flys. A well-intentioned person will sometimes say to you, "Have faith." If faith were such an accessible commodity why are we such a spiritually-hungry people? Perhaps faith emerges because we humans can look back and reflect. We see, in a lifetime of strung-together experiences—many of which would have felled a lesser soul—that we have endured. We did not endure because we had faith. We find faith because we endure.

Nancy Burke

Footnotes for Life

Be like the bird, who halting in his flight on limb too slight, yet sings–knowing he has wings.

Victor Hugo

I experienced blackouts in my drinking. Often I would wake up and not know where I had been, what I had said or done. I would peer through windows searching for my car. I would telephone to find out what time I had left the party and if anything had happened. Often as I bathed I would discover bruises or bleeding from an unremembered incident. There were other times I knew what I had done, knew what I had said, remembered how I behaved—and yet still I went back for more. I drank alcoholically for years because my pride would not allow me to be alcoholic. I created the wisest excuses for staying sick! Today my sobriety requires a wisdom that is based on reality.

> *It is human nature to think wisely and act foolishly.*
>
> Anatole France

Father Leo Booth

Footnotes for Life

_____

_____

_____

_____

_____

_____

_____

_____

I t took me a long time to understand what people meant when they said, "God speaks to me through other people." I wondered why I wasn't hearing any earth-shattering advice or wisdom from on high. Then I opened my mind, and my ears, to the experience, strength and hope all around me. My Higher Power was trying to speak to me, at meetings, through my sponsor, even through friends not in recovery, but I was refusing to listen. My willingness to see the divine in everyone is rewarded with precisely the wisdom and strength I seek. Today, may I be willing to open my heart to divine wisdom all around me.

*Love truth,
but pardon error.*

Voltaire

Amy Ellis

Footnotes for Life

_____

_____

_____

_____

_____

_____

_____

NOVEMBER 29

There is a new order in my life that allows me to fully experience love and excitement, peacefulness and harmony. I have important and worthwhile things to do. My life has meaning, even in the minutest details. My sense of purpose allows my energy and power to flow, and my purpose in life is to reveal the nature of my higher self in whatever I do. Within myself there exists all I need for this day, and every one that follows, to be one of fulfillment and success. As the sun sets, I can be content, knowing that I am deserving of rest and peaceful solitude to renew my spirit for the day to come.

Rokelle Lerner

There are many things we are capable of, that we could be or do. The possibilities are so great that we never are more than one-fourth fulfilled.

Katherine Anne Porter

Footnotes for Life

_____

_____

_____

_____

_____

_____

_____

_____

Happiness is an inside job. It comes from within me—something that I express and share. And contrary to what I learned through most of my life, its presence is not dependent on things "out there."

So, as I learn to take full responsibility for the way I feel about, and react to, people and situations, I begin to consciously create my life experiences. In the process, I come to understand that in order for me to be happy no one has to behave himself, nothing has to go "right," and no one has to love me—except me.

People are about as happy as they make up their minds to be.

Abraham Lincoln

Jeff McFarland

Footnotes for Life

_____

_____

_____

_____

_____

_____

_____

_____

Recovery is not about getting well, it is about getting real. When I was active in my disease I couldn't tell real from unreal. I was constantly swayed by lies, a void of truth within myself. When I pay attention to what I feel, what I perceive, what I know deep in my gut, I value my own being and I find that I can no longer be fooled. Here lies my strength. Here lies my freedom. I step confidently into my life.

Anna Joy Grace

Courage is the form of every virtue at the testing point, which means, at the point of highest reality.

C.S. Lewis

Footnotes for Life

_____

_____

_____

_____

_____

_____

_____

_____

DECEMBER 2

Strength: noun . . . .
spreading hope where there is doubt, love where there is hate, standing through trials, working through pain, getting up when you fall down, spreading joy where there is grief, and forgiving where forgiveness is absent.

Sarah Boesing

*Life only demands
from you the strength
you possess. Only one
feat is possible—not to
have run away.*

Dag Hammarskjold

Footnotes for Life

_____

_____

_____

_____

_____

_____

_____

Push yourself like a machine and you will eventually run low on energy. Love your mind by allowing it spaces of silence and it will serve you tirelessly. Notice how your senses are connected to your mind. Anything negative they pick up or generate will disturb the mind's workings. To maintain peace of mind, use your eyes, ears and mouths with care.

Brahma Kumaris
World Spiritual University

Rather than become a judge of others, become an advocate of their dreams.

Brahma Kumaris

Footnotes for Life

_____

_____

_____

_____

_____

_____

_____

_____

DECEMBER 4

I was sitting in a meeting at a very low point in my life, not knowing where to turn. Despair occupied every fiber of my being when the room suddenly disappeared and I was floating in an all-encompassing white light. There was no fear, no sadness, only unconditional love flowing around and through me. Then a voice that was an incredibly comforting presence told me to take what I needed. I had no idea what that might be but I knew I would find it. When the room came back into focus I was left with a tiny speck of that white light in my heart and the word "hope" in my mind and soul.

Hope can be miraculous!

Michael Jordan Segal

Anne Tiller Slates

Footnotes for Life

_____

_____

_____

_____

_____

_____

_____

DECEMBER 5

Wile as human beings are all in the same boat and are all on the same journey we know as life. Wouldn't it be nice if we could join hands in this journey and help each other through the struggles and challenges and together as a whole enjoy our successes?

Reach out your hand today and experience the peace and ecstasy of uniting with the human race as we collectively live together and help one another. The essence of spirituality is our connection with the world around us.

Richard Singer

I expect to pass through this world but once. Any good thing, therefore, that I can do or any kindness I can show to any fellow human being let me do it now.

Stephen Grellet

Footnotes for Life

_____

_____

_____

_____

_____

_____

_____

_____

DECEMBER 6

There are strangers who live around me. People I work with every day. Neighbors who sleep each night in houses close by. A grandmother. My own children. What do they think? How do they feel? We live side by side but we know so little about each other. It's time to look into the eyes of human beings who mow the lawn, use the office coffee pot or who sit on the other side of our own supper table. There is no greater tragedy than to live next to the treasure of another soul and never even look inside.

Renee Hixson

Life is too great of an adventure to live it indecisively. I'd rather step out in faith, take a risk and make a decision.

Renee Hixson

Footnotes for Life

As a child, I was sometimes ignored—even abused. It was too risky to show myself to the world so I hid my true self and found safety—refuge in invisibility. Now as an adult, I've discovered that too often I am invisible to myself. I ignore my needs, deny my emotions and I don't risk showing people who I really am. If I come out of hiding I can participate fully in life without fear of punishment or other negative consequences. I no longer have to be a victim of my biography.

Rokelle Lerner

The kindest way of helping yourself is to find a friend.

Ann Kaiser Stearns

Footnotes for Life

DECEMBER 8

As I began the wonderful journey into recovery, I realized the paradoxical beauty of my "powerlessness" over alcohol. I was unaware of the exacerbating factors that fueled my familial predisposition to alcoholism; my declaration of my "powerlessness" was replaced with a vigorous sense of responsibility to myself and my family generations to come. As I kept a daily journal, I developed a great deal of insight, which increased my desire to do my part in breaking the devastating cycle of addiction within my family. It was high time for me to become an advocate and leave behind the role of victim forever.

Sobriety and recovery are not just about abstaining from alcohol, but more importantly about taking responsibility.

Brenda L. Petite Ridgeway

Brenda L. Petite Ridgeway

Footnotes for Life

It was a stress-filled time and I was happy to have a cup of tea with my friend George. Being ninety-five years of age, he held the answers to all my unspoken questions. Sculptor and artist, George had escaped the Russian Revolution, leaving behind a home of considerable wealth. His family had been murdered by the Bolsheviks and he had fled by foot across Europe, carrying only memories.

Sensing my despair, George took my hands and, with deep emotion, boomed, "Look out another window! If you don't like what you see in your life, then find another view!"

Man is made by his belief. As he believes, so he is.

Bhagavad-Gita

Since that afternoon I have been looking through other windows, and I like what I see.

Irene Budzynski

Footnotes for Life

Anger was fashionable in the seventies. Otherwise-normal people spent hours screaming at and punching pillows. Fortunately, encounter groups soon went the way of disco. Letting go of unhealthy behavior is difficult work. Getting a handle on anger, with its delicious rush of self-righteousness, is particularly hard. Many of us cling to a kind of quiet fury, and at its worst, it batters the heart, sullies the soul and is altogether enervating. I don't know how much anger contributed to my own bad health, but it surely hurt my recovery. Practicing not getting angry a day at a time has been a tough job. I have found only two antidotes to anger: forgiveness and walking away.

Nancy Burke

Footnotes for Life

> *I internalize everything. I can't express anger; I grow a tumor instead.*
>
> Woody Allen

Sometimes when we're scared, all we want to do is hide from the world. But when we do this, our fears just get bigger. Isolation doesn't nurture recovery. Stay connected to people in simple ways; go to the mall, make light conversation with someone in a coffee shop, take a class or attend a free lecture at a bookstore. Come out of your shell so the world can show you love and how much you deserve happiness.

Lisa Jo Barr

*When you are alone
you are all your own.*

Leonardo da Vinci

Footnotes for Life

_____

_____

_____

_____

_____

_____

_____

DECEMBER 12

I believe in the dignity of every soul. Like a fine antique, addicts have a patina. They may be broken and need a bit of salvaging, but there is beauty under the surface, qualities that endure hardship and abuse, and a presence born of history and value. By showing compassion and kindness, by seeing the potential, not the past, I can make a difference in the life of every person I encounter.

Peter Vegso

To laugh often and much; to find the best in others; to leave the world a bit better, to know even one life has breathed easier because you have lived—this is to have succeeded.

Ralph Waldo Emerson

Footnotes for Life

DECEMBER 13

The catharsis of laughter can be just as powerful and transforming as the catharsis of tears or anger. To laugh with my entire being—to really get the joke and the joy of it all—is an unforgettable experience, one that leaves me forever a little different. Laughter is a symphony to the soul, and those we truly laugh with become special kinds of friends. When I cannot laugh, I cannot be. It means that I am so rigidly locked within myself that no air can get in. When I laugh, everything sort of loosens up inside, flies around and settles back down in an easier place. I remind myself that it is important to cry and equally so to laugh.

No man who has once heartily and wholly laughed can be altogether irreclaimably bad.

Thomas Carlyle

Tian Dayton

Footnotes for Life

_____

_____

_____

_____

_____

_____

_____

_____

DECEMBER 14

I keep wishing and hoping that someone I know and love will change. Whatever I want them to do, I have no power over their choices. I cannot change anyone but myself. Only by taking care of my own "stuff" can I make a difference in my world thus becoming a happier, healthier person. Just for today, God, I'll try to keep my side of the street clean; they'll have to sweep theirs all by themselves.

Sallie A. Rodman

The one unchangeable certainty is that nothing is unchangeable or certain.

John F. Kennedy

Footnotes for Life

_____

_____

_____

_____

_____

_____

_____

Self-respect is not a matter of what you are doing in your life, but rather of how you are doing it. It requires that you bring quality and virtue into each action, whatever that action may be. Sometimes you must burrow to find the good qualities in your nature that have gone underground and then coax them to the surface. Stopping for a moment and being silent can bring the steadiness you need for this task.

Brahma Kumaris
World Spiritual University

The world is your garden from which you remove weeds of doubt and replace them with seeds of hope.

Brahma Kumaris

Footnotes for Life

_____

_____

_____

_____

_____

_____

_____

_____

DECEMBER 16

I will imagine a dream fulfilled right now, this moment. I will see the table prepared before me. Life means to support me in the realization of my desires. It will move in and help if I can truly allow myself to see and feel that what I wish for is possible and indeed ready to be. Over and over again, I will visualize the circumstance that I wish to have in my life. I will mentally interact with it as if it were real. I will accept it as possible for me as if it were actually happening right now. Then I will let it go. I will see in my mind what I wish to see manifest in my life.

Tian Dayton

Only those who have, receive.

Joseph Roux

Footnotes for Life

_____

_____

_____

_____

_____

_____

_____

_____

I f I am to grow into the awesome promise of my life, I must embrace the truth that I am not a victim, except by my own choosing. Yes, painful things have happened in my life, but there is a big difference between feeling the pain and wallowing in it.

In fact, if I listen to my pain it will tell me where I have beliefs that no longer serve me, where I need to set healthy limits and boundaries, and where I have given away the power to decide how I will feel about the events, relationships and circumstances of my life.

Jeff McFarland

Man is equally incapable of seeing the nothingness from which he emerges and the infinity in which he is engulfed.

Blaise Pascal

Footnotes for Life

_____

_____

_____

_____

_____

_____

_____

_____

DECEMBER 18

Money isn't something to fear. It isn't the root of all evil. With a good attitude, money improves living. In recovery, we change our attitudes and find joy in money. As we prosper, we can help those around us prosper as well. Ideas and creative thoughts flow from us as we direct our energies toward specific goals. Money can be one of those goals. It is a powerful source of success when that wheel of fortune starts spinning around in our favor. It is a magnificent feeling and a divine right. Being comfortable with money helps us be confident, have fun, affect and infect those around us with positive attitudes.

Wine maketh merry; but money assureth all things.

Ecclesiastes 10:19

Yvonne Kaye

Footnotes for Life

_____

_____

_____

_____

_____

_____

_____

_____

For this alcoholic there is great irony in the choice of words when we talk about choosing to look at the glass half empty or half full. But choosing the optimistic approach makes all of the difference in every day of my recovery. A good day starts out with me remembering how far I've come and how strong I am. It is easy for me to get wrapped up in any problem du jour but then I see someone on the street, down and out, panhandling, drunk, and I am reminded that my problems today are luxurious compared to those I struggled with as an active alcoholic. I have a new lease on life, a second chance. I am forever grateful!

Perspective has helped me to see there is no way to happiness. Happiness is the way.

Stonewall Jackson

Dorri Olds

Footnotes for Life

_____

_____

_____

_____

_____

_____

_____

_____

DECEMBER 20

Today I will open myself to healing in my relationships. So much of life depends on the quality of intimacy with myself and so much of the quality of my intimacy is the quality of my relationships. It is synergistic. As my relationship with myself and my Higher Power gets better, my other relationships grow. Deep healing with people I care about has much more significance than might appear; it is soul and life-transforming. I experience moments of quiet expansion when my heart and mind actually feel as if they are widening in all directions. I am willing to grow a step at a time and heal little by little.

Life is not living, but living in health.

Martial

Tian Dayton

Footnotes for Life

_____

_____

_____

_____

_____

_____

_____

"So, it's been six weeks, Mom. How long do you suppose it's going to last this time?" Stunned, I looked deep into the eyes of my ten-year-old son. I saw skepticism, pain and disgust at my recent attempt at sobriety. He had heard it all before when I assured him numerous times that I would stop getting drunk.

Today, I have the privilege of looking that same, trusting son in the eye as I have every day since that night of reckoning. I have earned credibility. I am responsible. I will reassure him and he will hug me tightly! This time, I will say, "It's been twenty years, son! It's going to last."

Janell H.

> *There will come a time when you believe everything is finished. That will be the beginning.*
>
> Louis L'Amour

Footnotes for Life

_____

_____

_____

_____

_____

_____

_____

_____

DECEMBER 22

When traumatic events shake the foundations of your life, get out into the natural world—God will speak to you through his handiwork. Walk in solitude, drink in the regenerating air, open your senses to creation and take a lesson from nature. The healing in my life began when I came upon a field of fireweed while hiking. This magnificent wildflower shoots forth in splendor after an area is ravaged by fire; its magenta plumes wave proudly in stark contrast to its burned-out surroundings. The image opened my eyes, and I took what I learned from that moment to rise up from the ashes and go forth stronger and more alive than ever.

And hark! How blithe the throstle sings! He, too, is no mean preacher. Come forth into the light of things, let nature be your teacher.

William Wordsworth

Linda Mehus-Barber

Footnotes for Life

December 23

Feelings flirt with our desires while faith nurtures our needs. Feelings focus on the moment while faith concentrates on the future. Feelings flourish in immediate gratification while faith is willing to wait for what's better. Feelings react without thinking while faith takes the time and the thought to respond. Feelings are fickle and fleeting while faith considers the long run. Feelings want only to receive while faith decides to believe. What feelings do I still allow to control me? What can I choose to place my faith in today to better serve my true needs tomorrow?

Faith can take us farther than any of our feelings.

Anne Calodich Fone

Anne Calodich Fone

Footnotes for Life

_____

_____

_____

_____

_____

_____

_____

_____

DECEMBER 24

I suffered much from the effects of my loved one's addiction. Disappointments, manipulation, emotional abuse and betrayal dimmed my will to live. It was hard just to keep going. After all this, surely I am not expected to forgive! I let go of my old definition of forgiveness. I consider this—forgiveness is not about letting someone who hurt me off the hook. It is about letting me off the hook. I can feel, heal, express and live in the joy of this moment. I know I have forgiven when the cloud of past hurt no longer blocks today's sun. In what part of my life do I welcome more sunshine today?

Anna Joy Grace

It is easier to forgive an enemy than to forgive a friend.

William Blake

Footnotes for Life

_____

_____

_____

_____

_____

_____

_____

_____

The Christmas tree was destroyed; presents were smashed; our father was drunk, but for a moment, one brief moment, none of it mattered. My nine-year-old brother shot up out of bed like a rocket, took in a sharp breath and said, "Listen, reindeer!" So I listened silently to the scraping on the roof, something more magical than the familiar sound of squirrels. Staring at my brother, I saw something amazing—a smile. When belief and awe sparkled in his aqua eyes, for that moment in time, I, too, believed in the miracle of Christmas. Those heart-wrenching holidays are a distant nightmare, but I remember the gift I received that Christmas—a gift of hope.

Raquel M. Strand

Footnotes for Life

Do what you can, with what you have, where you are.

Theodore Roosevelt

I am on a journey of spirit. Spirit calls to me within and without. In a still, small voice I sense spirit whispering in my inner ear. My body feels an increasing sense of aliveness as I invite spirit to make itself known. Spirit breathes in each pore within me. It fills the numbness with energy. It fills the emptiness and causes my inner being to overflow with its presence. Whenever I become still and allow spirit to enter my world, it is always there waiting for me to discover it, to remember it, to invite it in.

Tian Dayton

On a long journey of human life, faith is the best of companions; it is the best refreshment on the journey; and it is the greatest property.

Buddha

Footnotes for Life

_____

_____

_____

_____

_____

_____

_____

The door through the darkness is human touch. We do not need to see the light if we can hold a hand. A hug speaks languages that have no letters and need no translators. A gentle embrace can acknowledge sorrows too deep to speak aloud. When loneliness builds an island far away from hope it is not a land alone. The touch of one caring soul can build a bridge of hope, healing and a sense of belonging. We need not be eloquent or brilliant or even totally whole. We just need to care enough to reach out and touch another soul.

Renee Hixson

To touch the soul of another human being is to walk on holy ground.

Stephen Covey

Footnotes for Life

_____

_____

_____

_____

_____

_____

_____

_____

DECEMBER 28

It is our children who will reap the consequences of our endeavors to find ourselves. It is the truth that lies within us that they often see us avoid or confront. It is they who gain wisdom from the truth we tell ourselves, the failures we refuse to acknowledge, the mountains we climb and the summit we reach.

Betty King

As the bird sits in its nest and the winds blow, it is the safety of its eggs the robin is concerned with, for it is the next generation the future owns.

Betty King

Footnotes for Life

_____

_____

_____

_____

_____

_____

_____

One of the best gifts I can give a person is my full attention when they need someone to listen. Truly listening is an unselfish act. Without saying a word, we can give the gift of insight and perspective to someone who is struggling with a problem, processing the changes in their lives or thinking through a new idea. For best reception, tune in. There is no need to offer advice. All we need to do is open our minds and hearts to hear what is being said.

Sherrie M. Johnston

Listening, not imitation, may be the sincerest form of flattery.

Dr. Joyce Brothers

Footnotes for Life

_____

_____

_____

_____

_____

_____

_____

_____

DECEMBER 30

I understand that recovery is many little acts and subtle changes in attitudes. Recovery is not talking differently—it is being different. I will follow through on plans that I make and keep my life simple. I will not allow abuse in my home, of me or anyone else. I will take a positive attitude toward my life. Recovery is not only about reworking my past—it is about not repeating it. It is the little steps I actually take that count. A small inner change, if it is real, can have a more transforming effect than a large outer one. Setting impossible, unreachable goals for myself is just another way to stay sick. Doing something small well will give me self-respect and serenity.

Our health is our sound relation to external objects; our sympathy with external being.

Ralph Waldo Emerson

Tian Dayton

Footnotes for Life

Y ou are a unique individual with gifts; to dream, to become, to use your talents and to realize your potential. Build your life's dream by reaching out with love, inspiration, forgiveness and selflessness. Touch the souls of people. Make a difference with unbridled enthusiasm and a positive approach. You might just be able, through example, to transform someone else's dream into a reality.

George H. Moffett

Dream as if you'll live forever, live as if you'll die today.

James Dean

Footnotes for Life

_____

_____

_____

_____

_____

_____

_____

_____

Carla Edmisten, ©2005 Carla Edmisten.

Amy Ellis, ©2005 Amy Ellis.

Lana Fletcher, ©2005 Lana Fletcher.

Anne Calodich Fone, ©2005 Anne Calodich Fone.

Darlene Franklin, ©2005 DarleneFranklin.

John C. Friel, Ph.D. reprinted from *Chicken Soup for the Recovering Soul* ©2004 Jack Canfield and Mark Victor Hansen, published by Health Communications, Inc.

Valerie Frost, ©2005 Valerie Frost.

Michelle Gipson, ©2005 Michelle Gipson.

Anna Joy Grace, ©2005 Anna Joy Grace.

Vicki Graf, ©2005 Vicki Graf.

Carol Davis Gustke reprinted from *Chicken Soup for the Recovering Soul* ©2004 Jack Canfield and Mark Victor Hansen, published by Health Communications, Inc.

Janell H. reprinted from *Chicken Soup for the Recovering Soul* ©2004 Jack Canfield and Mark Victor Hansen, published by Health Communications, Inc.

Erin Hagman reprinted from *Chicken Soup for the Recovering Soul* ©2004 Jack Canfield and Mark Victor Hansen, published by Health Communications, Inc.

Karen Hall, ©2005 Karen Hall.

Joyce Harvey, ©2003 Joyce Harvey.

Shary Hauer, ©2005 Shary Hauer.

Debbie Heaton reprinted from *Chicken Soup for the Recovering Soul* ©2004 Jack Canfield and Mark Victor Hansen, published by Health Communications, Inc.

Maryellen Heller, ©2005 Maryellen Heller.

Miriam Hill reprinted from *Chicken Soup for the Recovering Soul* ©2004 Jack Canfield and Mark Victor Hansen, published by Health Communications, Inc.

Renee Hixson, ©2005 Renee Hixson.

Alexandra P., ©2005 Alexandra P.

Theresa Peluso reprinted from *Chicken Soup for the Recovering Soul* ©2004 Jack Canfield and Mark Victor Hansen, published by Health Communications, Inc.

Ava Pennington, ©2005 Ava Pennington.

Maribeth Pittman, ©2005 Maribeth Pittman.

Kay Conner Pliszka, ©2005 Kay Conner Pliszka. Passage on September 18th, reprinted from *Chicken Soup for the Recovering Soul* ©2004 Jack Canfield and Mark Victor Hansen, published by Health Communications, Inc.

Felice Prager, ©2004 Felice Prager.

Reiki Principle excerpt is in the public domain. Reiki is an ancient Japanese technique that balances the life force energy by the laying on of hands which promotes healing, stress reduction and relaxation.

Peggy Reeves, ©2005 Peggy Reeves.

Carol McAdoo Rehme, ©2005 Carol McAdoo Rehme.

Jennifer M. Reinsch reprinted from *Chicken Soup for the Recovering Soul* ©2004 Jack Canfield and Mark Victor Hansen, published by Health Communications, Inc.

Naomi Rhode reprinted from *Chicken Soup for the Nurse's Soul* ©2001 Jack Canfield and Mark Victor Hansen, published by Health Communications, Inc.

Brenda Ridgeway, ©2005 Brenda Ridgeway.

Carla Riehl reprinted from *Chicken Soup for the Recovering Soul* ©2004 Jack Canfield and Mark Victor Hansen, published by Health Communications, Inc.

Sallie A. Rodman, ©2005 Sallie A. Rodman. Passage on February 20th reprinted from *Chicken Soup for the Recovering Soul* ©2004 Jack Canfield and Mark Victor Hansen, published by Health Communications, Inc.

Thom Rutledge, ©2004 ThomRutledge. Adpated from an article originally appearing in The Phoenix.

TOPIC INDEX

Please enjoy this book day-by-day or select a particular topic that will inspire you from the index below.

TOPIC INDEX

Topic Index

Topic Index